May God bless you
always
Willie Murth
P.T.L.

BLACK AND TRYING

BLACK AND TRYING

By Willie Murphy

NEW LEAF
PRESS

Harrison, Arkansas

Library of Congress Catalog Card Number: 76-22272
International Standard Book Number: 0-89221-023-0

Dedication

This book is dedicated to my Mom and Dad whom God gave to me as spiritual leaders and, also, appreciation to my grandmother who is with the Lord and who prayed daily that God would save her whole household. She claimed Acts 16:31 for her family and God answered prayer. Amen.

Mom and Dad

CONTENTS

FOREWORD

This is a story about a black man. From the most humble beginnings we will see a true story of holiness and honor unfold. Willie Murphy has gone through, not the evolution, but the revolution, from servant of man to servant of self, to servant of God. There never was a stranger heart given among men than the heart of Willie Murphy. From a heart of festering pride, to a heart of fervent praise, from a life of impossible circumstances to a life of miraculous circumstances—this is Willie Murphy's story.

You will enjoy the special relationship of the Murphy family. Their relationship with one another and with their God touches the humiliating, the hilarious, the holy, the happy, the honorable.

It is fitting that this story should be printed in black and white, for much of the tale lies therein. Facing the accusations of living in a white man's world and serving a white man's God, Willie has tenaciously, but tenderly lived this modern Gospel epic.

The life of Willie Murphy could have made him bitter, but instead it made him better. The reader will find himself a benefactor of this betterness and will in turn be better for having read the story of this bombastic black Bartholomew.

Jim Spillman

PREFACE

I pray that this book in giving these details will be a guideline to many people that they not be caught in the problems I was, and that they might know the road-signs.

I knew the roadsigns.

I knew the stop-sign point, but I allowed myself to go beyond those stopping points.

God has told us that He has made a way of escape. There is no temptation that will befall us but that He will make a way of escape. But I allowed myself to go beyond those temptation points. I allowed and so I can't blame the devil. I cannot even blame God.

All the tragedies that happened in my Christian life have not made me turn from my Lord, but it's made me even stronger—made me want to go out and minister.

I'm beginning to learn the meaning of the word "friend."

A friend is not someone who leaves you when things are bad. A friend isn't someone who says I'm a friend only when things are going well—when things are good, when you are shining and when things are bright.

A friend is someone who sticks closer than a brother. Of course, that friend is Jesus. If we are Christians we're not only supposed to be a friend to another Christian brother or sister only in good times. Christ would never turn his back on me or you. No matter whether we were flying high or whether we had fallen. He would always be there with outstretched hands to welcome us, to help us. God expects us to be the same way.

8

I've had many people who've said, "Hey, I'm your friend," when things are going well. "I'm your brother. We really love you." But the minute I had fallen, the minute things went wrong for me those same ones who said, "I'm your friend. We love you. We'll stick by you," turned their backs.

When we become Christians God expects something from us. God does different things for us even when we are wrong. Even when we're bad, God still leaves room. He leaves the door open that we can come and be forgiven, and He still loves us. He expects the same things of us.

Ofttimes we condemn people, and sometimes we don't even know why, and God forgives us for this, but He expects when we find out that we've been wrong to go and make amends and to ask for forgiveness of those concerned.

There are so many people who say they are Christians but they have this deep prejudice—so deep that Jesus can't be seen. I don't believe we have reached the point yet to see answered what Jesus prayed in John 17: 22, "That they may be one, even as we are one." I pray that it will be the same with that love that you and I share, that we too will have this same love. I know I haven't reached that yet, but I want to.

The reason for writing this book is that some love, that some right can be shown where race relations are concerned. Where somehow Christian brothers and sisters can get along with Jesus. How what we feel, what we act, what we see, what we say, all that has a lasting effect on others may be truly Christian. And that if anything that can come out of all of this that is written, that it can open some eyes. Then I will praise God for it.

—Willie Murphy

Chapter 1
Life on the Plantation

The place where I was born is called Hope Hull, Alabama. Don't look for it on the map because you won't find it. Well, maybe!

It was a community or plantation. The farmers owned several hundred acres on this plantation. There were approximately eight or ten families who lived in the section where we lived. We all knew each other and were real close friends and relatives.

As my Dad put it, as far back as we can trace our folk were born on this plantation—my grandfather and all his folk. I was only ten days old when my grandfather died. My love for music possibly came to me from him.

At that time there were but few instruments of music such as organs or pianos. Grandfather owned an organ. His home was often the meeting place of the young people of the community. He would play and sing and everyone had a joyful time. His oldest daughter, Mamie, had never studied music but when the rich whites of the community had social affairs they always had Mamie to play for them. It was said by many, especially whites, including music teachers, that no one

11

could get as much music out of an organ or piano as Mamie. Anything you could sing, classical, or what have you, she could play if sung once for her. The old folks would often gather together after picking cotton all day and sing. Sometimes we would build a big fire and sing around it. It was a happy relationship.

Sometimes we had hog-killing time. All the neighbors would come together and kill hogs. My dad did most of the hog-killing. Sometimes he would go to the other farms and help them kill their hogs. Many times we shared hog corpses. Most of these people were just poor—one-hundred percent poor! But it was a happy joyful time for me as a little boy.

My father had this to say about my grandfather James Murphy, who was also the butcher for the community: "He supplied all the people of the community with beef and pork for their weekend meals and festive occasions. He would take orders all week and deliver his orders on Friday and Saturday. He was a man of unusual physical strength. His first wife passed after the birth of two children—both girls. His second marriage was to my grandmother, Arebella Grant. To this union was born one girl and two boys. James, the older, was my father. Willie, the younger was a school teacher."

Dad always had an ambition to do something but we lived on this man's property who owned the general store, and we share-cropped.

We worked hard all year. To buy feed, clothes, and food we had to go to the general store. The white merchants would let the Negro farmers have food, a few clothes and fertilizer from March through August of each year at fifty cents on the dollar. After the crops were gathered there would be a settlement between the land owner, the merchant and the farmer or share-cropper. The blacks kept no records except in a very few cases. For the most part they believed what the white man said was true. The majority were told upon the settlement at the end of the harvest time: "Well, Sam, you did well this year. You almost paid out, you only owe. . ." (whatever they wanted to tell you). For instance, they might say, "$150 or more and I'll add this to next year's amount at fifty cents on the dollar." The fifty cents on the dollar meant that the $150 had immediately grown to $225, plus whatever you had to have for the next year at fifty cents on the dollar. In most cases there was no way out. You were kept in debt from year to year. Right or wrong, you could not dispute a white man's word. This meant you had to stay where you were unless someone paid your balance. If the land-owner liked you pretty well and you made a good crop you could get anything a black might need, but at an enormous cost.

We didn't have money so we had to make a loan from this general store and at harvest time we would sell what we had grown all year to pay our bill at the store, and consequently we wound up with no money. It was a year-in year-out thing.

My dad had two or three little churches that he was pastoring and he would sometimes leave home on Thursday or Friday and wouldn't return until Monday or Tuesday. He never came home with any greenbacks. In those days you weren't looking for black power, you were looking for green power. He always came home with some flour, meal, or chickens. Sometimes he was given some fatback but was seldom given any money. And if so he would give it back to the churches. The little wooden churches were so poor and needed money so badly for fixing up.

In those days religion was the biggest thing in the life of the black people. They believed in the baptism of the Holy Spirit, people falling out (prostrate) under the power of God's word. This often happened during the services. And when those so touched got up they had something to say. They believed in the sincerity of their religious leaders even though the majority of whom had no seminary training. The study of the Bible was not as evident as today, but there was a revelation given to many who took the time to pray for it.

Preachers were on both sides of my family. They loved the Lord with all their hearts and taught their children the same.

In those early days I don't know of a family that taught their children to hate. Today it's *let's get the whites,* or, *stop those blacks.*

We grew up in the church. That was all I knew—church, church, church.

I grew up hearing my dad say, "Kids, mind the older people." We were taught to say to them, "Yes, Sir. No, Sir." We were to respect everybody, whether black or white.

I was the baby of the family. As I grew older somehow I turned out bitter. It wasn't that I was taught it, it was just something that happened on the inside of me. It wasn't a thing that was so outward that you could see it but it was on the inside—something that I harbored there because I saw that white people had so much more than blacks.

One day while playing with a kid who happened to be a white boy who was perhaps eleven, said to me, "Hi, Willie!" I had gone into his house to get a glass of water and I called to him, "Hi, Johnny." He said, "Come on in." "May I get a glass of water in the kitch-

14

en." I had called him by his first name, His dad said, "Don't you ever call him Johnny, he is *Mr.* Johnny to you." "I'm not going to do it," I said. He was about to bop me across the head and said, "Either you do it or stay out of this house, and don't play with my son." I wasn't about to call him *Mister,* when I was 14!

I told my dad what happened and he said, "He is older than you and you should respect him, besides you were in his home. If he told you to call his son Mister, you should do it. It's not right that you do, but you should respect him because he is and adult. And besides, Christians should have respect one for another." I still thought it ridiculous. But Dad was trying to teach me a lesson. He meant well. He didn't want me run over by any other man, but he wanted me to respect that man because he was older, and I was in his home.

Anyway, this kid made a joke of it. He came to me and said, "Now don't you forget that I'm 'Mr.' to you." When he said this we went into a big fight, and then we got up and made up. We were buddies again.

Things like this happened in my young life and each instance seemed to take me further and further away from my white friends.

An incident that played a large part in my life was the story of a beautiful homesite given my grandfather. He was well-known and well-liked in the community and was given this land by a very wealthy white family. It was his land as long as he lived.

My Dad filled me in on this story.

A white family wanted this land. They came one night and tricked grandfather into getting into a car. Granddad was to go and approve or recommend a black man whom this white farmer supposedly wanted to hire.

15

When he got into the car the white man put a gun to his side and drove to a forest swamp and had him get out and marched him to a group of 30 to 40 hooded Ku Klux Klansmen. After much discussion they gave him the privilege to leave the acreage and never come back, or be killed. He consented to leave. They told him he could go north or south. He decided to go south. He was taken by the white man to a white lady land-owner who purchased his ticket to New Orleans, Louisiana. Then he was escorted to the train and guarded there until the train signalled to pull out.

At the time there was a law that if the owner wasn't found in three weeks it was free land and anyone could grab it. The whites claimed it and to this day the land is still in their family.

Everything the man had was taken. The family was left in misery for days not knowing whether their father was dead or alive. After a few days he came back to Montgomery and hid around until he could contact his family, and then left for Birmingham where he hid around for quite some time. He was sought by a poor class of whites who do the dirty work of the rich for any escapee. Finally his health failed and he came back to Hope Hull. No one attempted to disturb him. He died in peace at the age of 57.

My folks prayed and read the Bible all the time. However, I got further and further away from the Bible and Christianity because of some folk who were such good "Christians," but to me didn't exemplify the Christian life, and also they lived in poverty. I didn't want any part of it. To myself I said: *When I get to be a man I'm getting out of this southland!*

Other stories that disturbed me was of the white man against the black in man's inhumanity to man in

16

a number of shootings.

Again, my Dad related to me this event:

On the farm we lived a section was used by the whites to bait several acres for doves. Many doves came from all around and fed there. Huntsmen would gather there and kill doves just at dawn and until around seven or eight in the morning.

Just a mile from our home four Negro men were called out from their homes between midnight and daylight by a Negro man—one of their neighbors who was forced to do so by the whites. We heard the firing of the guns that riddled their bodies with the shots. Three of the men fell on top of the fourth. Fearing detection and thinking they had killed all four, the assassins hurriedly left at the break of day.

In less than an hour the news reached us. Those assassinated were Harry Russell and his two sons. The fourth lived some fifty or more years after this and was called Kit Jackson. The reason for the shooting: they were accused of poisoning two or more horses belonging to a white family living in the community.

I knew the family who had been shot. It disturbed me greatly. I got more bitter. I shouldn't have hated but I did. I think I hated mainly because I didn't know Jesus at the time. You either live by Jesus or you live by the devil. At the time I didn't want to be a Christian. I was being led by the devil without knowing it.

As a youngster I never had clothes of my own. They were always hand-me-downs. There were four brothers. You can imagine what those clothes were like by the time they got to me! This too added to the series of instances that turned me away from wanting to be a Christian.

I was like many young people who are putting up

fronts. Kids who were brought up in church and because their parents are in the church were supposed to be good examples of child obedience but they can't succeed because the parents don't know they are doing all kinds of things on the side. At home they are smiling. Mom and Dad think everything is just fine.

I decided at an early age I was going to get an education—I promised my folks. The white folks were the ones who could read. The reason the blacks couldn't read was because they had to work and couldn't go to school. White people didn't work in the south. They didn't do farming—that was mostly done by the black people.

School for the blacks was taught over a three-to-four-month period, beginning in October or November, and closing around the first or second week in March. Often during those months many of the black children were kept out of school to pick cotton, much of which was not completed until February. Many were poorly clothed and the cold winter weather made it very difficult to do a full days work. When not in school we had to work, we had to have money.

The school was a one-room log cabin, more or less, and was for all blacks. There would be six grades in one building, with one teacher for all six grades. That was adequate because there would probably be only four or five students in each grade.

Most of the white land owners taught the parents of black children that their children did not need an education, and sending them to school was a waste of time, and tended to make them lazy. They stressed the need of teaching the black children to work with their hands.

I was disgusted with my upbringing by the time I

was 15 or 16. I was just beside myself, and yet, I put up a front to my parents.

My Methodist preacher-dad was transferred from time to time. By the time I was 15 he was transferred to a place called Greenville, Alabama. That is where I met my wife.

I started school there and the hatred that was in me wasn't so dominant at that time. I could forget and there would be times that it would come back and leave me with a real heaviness in my heart. But I was active in school in those days because I wanted to get an education. I wanted to be the best that I could be.

I also started to sing just a bit before moving to Greenville. One of my brothers was a tremendous singer. I wanted to be like him and to walk in his footsteps.

Even at six years of age I remember being out in the old barn singing my head off and having a good time, and I would begin to weep. Then I quit singing and forgot about it. A year or so would go by and I would find myself singing again. For hours upon hours—running across the field just singing. I told myself that when I got to be a man out of school I wanted to be a choir director for one thing.

My mom prayed that I would be a preacher before I was born and that was the thing that I was definitely *not* going to be. No way was I going to be a preacher! I thought I might do well as a choir director, or a school teacher, or teaching music in the school.

But God works in mysterious ways *His wonders* to perform.

Chapter 2
Northbound

The house we lived in was built by my dad. My grandfather and a couple of the men in the community cut the oak trees. Their axes were sharp on both ends. The boards were so thick that it took three men to lift one board. It was a three-room house, great big rooms. It had two doors, and two windows—that was all. It had a high-slanted ceiling, and, of course, was infested with snakes in the summer. In the winter and summer it was completely air-conditioned.

We had a big fireplace. One could stand in front of this fireplace to keep warm in the winter. You would freeze on the back side because the wind was coming in so freely.

Ususally my brothers, three or four of us, would sleep in the same bed. At six years of age we all had to work. And if from the time of four you could do anything you worked. One just didn't want to sit around knowing that everybody else was working. At six I worked in the cotton field picking cotton. Of course, everybody else was too—my brothers, my mom and dad, my grandmother, grandfather—all were cotton pickers. That's what we called them, because that was the way we earned our money.

If we share-cropped, it was our own cotton we picked, and we sold it by the bales and got the money for it. All the money somehow or other ended up at the general store because we had to buy food all year long.

In 1938 and 1939 the government came out with a proclamation that there was land for sale in a place called Gunners Hill, Alabama. This land would be sold to families like us—black families that didn't have any property. The land would sell for $12 an acre. When the proclamation came out, my dad was one of the first to go and purchase. He purchased 165 acres. We thought we were rich people. We didn't pay a dime for that land. It was no money down, just to work off the payments with the crops.

We moved out of the cotton fields in the deep south of Montgomery and moved to a place called Gunners Hill. It was a little closer to Montgomery, and everything was going great for us.

Now my dad actually owned a piece of property! There were other families that moved out of that last plantation area to this new area.

By the time we moved here my hatred strike was starting to fade because I was beginning to say that white people weren't all that bad. Look at what the governor's done for us now!

When the war broke out in 1941, my brother decided that he had to go to war so when he left there was only my two brothers and I on the farm. I was perhaps 13 at the time. It seemed I had to do all of the work and I didn't want to do it. I wanted to go fishing all the time. I didn't want to do that planting and plowing . . . it was cotton and we had beans and tomatoes coming out of our ears!

We had two mules to plow with. One was named Lily. When you plowed with Lily and Jack (Jack was a lazy one) you had to use everything you had to get him to go.

We got to raising lima beans and selling them. Things began to really look up. We were making a little money on our farm.

The government built a new home on this farm for us. It didn't have any lights and we used oil lamps. After being on that farm for a year a bill was passing that electric lines could be put up throughout the country and rural area. The line went in front of our house, and all of a sudden we had electric lights. I can remember sitting there all night looking at the lights and actually trying to blow them out. It wouldn't go out so I told Mama, "I can't get this light to go out."

In spite of all the good things that were happening for us there was something inside of me that was bugging me, an anxiety to get out of that situation. It was a good situation and I should have enjoyed it very much, but I just wanted to leave the south.

We still had to walk to school. That made me hate a little bit more. We walked eleven miles to the school in Gunners Hill, 12 or 13 of us, on a gravel road. No paved road then. We had to walk across the wooden bridges and swampy areas. There was a tiny creek winding through that area. I recall seeing the people on the school bus. The only people who rode school busses in those days were white kids, and, of course, they passed by us and they would scream at us, "Look at them niggers walking." That was 22 miles a day we had to walk. We thought we were having fun. Walking, laughing and having a great time.

Something good happened to us. Jeeps were made available, so my dad bought one.

When folk talked about the city and how plentiful money, jobs and food were, it really impressed my brothers to want to get out of this farm work. In fact, when we moved to that new area, Gunners Hill, my brothers (only two now) one went into the army, and the other moved to Pittsburgh, Pennsylvania. When they talked about the city and all the fun, I was the little boy and they would chase me out. When they weren't looking I'd stand at the door and listen to them anyway, and hear all the big things they talked about. All the talk of greatness of the city life, fanfare and all, burned a desire in my heart to get out of the south—get out of the country, and away from the farm.

As a young boy I remember this man who owned this large farm that was nearby. He had a black fellow who worked for him. He was a chauffer and wore a white hat and neat-looking suit. He would drive by while we were watching. I thought, *When I get to be a man I'm going to buy me a black car and I'm going to get me a white chauffer.* This, too, added hatred to my heart. I wanted to have what everyone else had.

My dad was always preaching the Gospel and talking about God loving us, and that we ought to love God because He has done so much for us. I said, "Well, God only loves the white people because look at what they have." I wanted to get away from the white people.

I wanted to go north. That's what I set my goal for. I figured if I was going to leave the south, I needed some kind of education so I decided to try to struggle through high school, and if I could get some college, fine.

Just before my sixteenth birthday my dad sold the farm and took a church in Greenville, Alabama. I was happy about getting rid of that farm. That farm land is now at the city limit of Montgomery. Papa gave it away. He sold 165 acres for $3,000. Now it is perhaps worth about $38 a square foot. It's a shame he did it because of us boys; we guys wouldn't stay there. I wanted to go because it was the city—just to get out of the country.

In those days school was either all black or all white. My idea was to get an education so I could leave the south some day. My folks didn't know that this burning thing was on the inside of me to better myself. They didn't know that I had this thing about white people because I could smile. I could fool just about anybody with a smile. At least that's what *I thought*.

I finished high school with a scholarship in music. I couldn't read a note, but I sang and won monetary scholarships in the school music choirs and group singings.

I started singing listening to my folks singing the old songs. My grandmother and grandfather on both sides sang, and, hearing them even though I was so small I could hardly remember hearing them perhaps four or so years of age, it was something that stuck in my heart. My mother, sister and grandmother all sang.

When I was told I could acquire a scholarship when I finished high school I began to search for a college to attend. A cousin told me of a college in North Carolina. *Hee, hee, that's "north"* I thought. Well, it wasn't "north" enough.

Up to this time I had generalized where the white people were concerned. White people were all crimesmen, I thought. All KKK hated black people. I had taken a few people and blamed the whole white race for the things that were done by just a few misguided unbelieving people.

I didn't know the Lord, I thought I did but I didn't. When I was about eight or nine years of age, I remember attending a revival meeting in our area. In this meeting was a preacher, super tall with long arms. I'll never forget this man in Jackson Prospect Baptist Church.

With a night out, a night to get away from home and from the work we all went to hear preaching on hell, fire and brimstone. I don't remember a word he preached but it was a frightening subject. I knew that when he finished preaching, hell was a bad place; it was *BAD*. The preacher had fiery eyes with brimstone just hanging out of each eyelid.

We had in those days what we call mourner's benches, the first two pews across the front. And all the sinner folks, folks who knew that they were sinners, just automatically, during a revival went up and sat in those front pews. I spent my young life on those two pews.

This tall preacher began to point that long finger. He seemed to point at me though there were ten or twelve of us on those front pews. He looked at us with fire in his eye and said, "You are going to hell if you don't stop your evil ways, your sinning. The devil is going to get you, and hell's a terrible place." He talked about hell as if he'd just gotten back, and he'd just really run that thing down to you.

I knew hell was bad and I didn't want to go. He said, "If you don't want to go to hell, you come up here and get saved. Come up to this altar." What else are you going to do, you don't want to go to hell, it's too bad. So he emptied those pews every night.

I'm sure something happened to some of those kids, adults as well, but nothing really happened in my heart. I just went because I was frightened. I was sprinkled in those days. When I shook the preacher's hand one Sunday morning, he quoted a few words, "Do you believe in God? Do you believe in the church?" I said, "Yes." And with that I thought I was a Christian.

I had a lot to learn because going to Greenville church school didn't teach much Bible. It was a regular school. We had to work like in a public school. Of course, we did have chapel. And we had Sunday school at the boarding school that I stayed in.

We had a good choir which I sang in and won many, many awards. It was a good Christian school, but seemed somewhat superficial. It was enough to just quote some words and you were a Christian.

I didn't know the Lord as I know Him today; and, consequently, with this hatred on the inside of me and not knowing the Lord, it led me to quite a few errors. John 10:10 speaks of "a thief comes but to rob and steal"—that's exactly what he had done for me because I had my mind made up that I was going to make something of my life and I was not going to be a preacher. I didn't even want to be a Christian if it was going to stop me from making something of my life. I wanted some green power not white power. I especially wanted to get away from white folk.

Before I finished high school I had met Mary. I had known her about two years now. *She ran after me for about two years!* (Smile!) *Everywhere I went, there was Mary, chasing me down. I stopped long enough for her to catch me.*

I decided if I was going to make it, when I got married right after finishing graduation from high school, that my chances were shot now.

I wanted to go to college. I had a scholarship. What was I to do? Rather than go to North Carolina as my grandmother had moved from there to Pittsburgh, Pennsylvania, and I thought there is more of a chance there, maybe.

I had a good job with Goodyear Tire and Recapping Company, recapping big truck tires—(10 to 20's)—and me a little slip of a fellow! They paid me $18 a week for working 10 hours a day, six days a week. When I got married, I got a raise—$24. I thought that wasn't going to be enough money and wanted to make a bit more. There was rebellion in my heart. With my grandmother in Pittsburgh I thought Pittsburgh was a good opportunity. And having married, I thought, *I am my own man.* What I wanted was "up north." I quit my job, and left Mary with her mother so I could look for a job.

After being in Pittsburgh three days, I was hired by a Jewish gentleman. I will never forget this. He looked at me, and said, "I want you to know that I don't hire anyone unless they live in the state, or, here in the community for some time and are established, because otherwise they may be worthless. You don't have any references. I don't know anything about you but you seem like a good fellow, a well-mannered fellow."

For the first time I began to see my folks' efforts of upbringing in my life. They had told us to respect older people. I was doing these things. He didn't hear this in the big city. Here it was Johnny, Joe and Jack. Nobody "Mistered" anyone. I said "Mr. Harris," "Yes, Sir," and "No, Sir." Because I was doing this he hired me.

I had a very good working relationship with Mr. Harris. He gave me a suit worth $125! All the clothes I had all my life up to that point weren't worth that much money. Then he gave me a beautiful grey shark-skin. (I had a zoot suit that I had been wearing but it was old now). I didn't want to accept the suits at first and said, "Mr. Harris, why are you doing it?" I thought it was a gimmic. No white people did anything for black people unless they wanted something in return. I said, "I don't believe I want to accept this, unless you tell me how I can pay you back." He said, "No, I did it because I really like you. I really, really appreciate you. I think you are a tremendous person. That's the only reason I gave it to you—no strings attached."

He kept doing things like this; buying furniture for our apartment. He gave me the money for my wife to take the bus from Alabama to Pittsburgh, and said, "Just because I like you I do it." He didn't want anything back. He gave us a complete outfit for each of the children when they were born and didn't want to be paid back. It was just because, "We like you, we really like you, we appreciate you." I had never had white people tell me that.

I was so bitter at that time, I couldn't shake hands with white people. I wasn't used to it and when people would shake hands with me (its such a small thing) and give me a sort of wet handshake, when they weren't watching, I just kind of wiped it off on my clothes . . . sneaky like because I thought I'd catch a disease from white people. I'm not sure they didn't feel the same way.

I was the most narrow-minded person and yet God had mercy, because my grandmother and my parents were praying. I know prayer changes things. They prayed in spite of what their children were doing. They were constantly on their knees for us. Grandma never ceased to pray.

I had a good job now and was paid a starting salary of $50. Imagine going from $18 or $24 to $50 a week! The little people in Alabama who were school teachers weren't making much more then that. I was paid all in $1 bills, and it was a *fat* stack.

My first paycheck came while my wife was still in Alabama. I wrote her: "Honey, you've got to come here. This is God's country. And the white folks here are not so bad." I sent her some of those $1 bills. I didn't even have sense enough to get a money order. About three months later my wife was in Pittsburgh.

But in spite of all the things that Mr. Harris did for me, and how much he told me he appreciated my work, (and I liked Mr. Harris) I was still not relating to white people. There was still something in me from those early days of all the mistreatment I had seen that had been done to my own personal family.

I was walking the streets of Montgomery one day and three white fellows were also walking up the street. It was on a Saturday, and usually the black folks after a hard week of work, would go to the city. They would take their wagons, load them up and go to the city. It was a big day for blacks. And here I am walking up the sidewalk and these three white fellows were walking there also and I had to step off in the street, and let them on the sidewalk, because they would not move over so I could walk by.

At another time I had been walking down the street and four white kids and their parents were sitting and gazing at me and said, "Look at the little black nigger. Look at him."

All these things were built up in me and something in me was rebelling against those days. I wanted to pay back everything that had ever happened to me—like having my grandfather chased out of the south.

Once there was a young 17-year-old fellow walking down the street and this lady was taking a bath with her windows open and shades pulled back. So when walking down the street and one hears water running one automatically looks to the sound. You are not peeking, it's just a natural thing to look. The windows in the south are pretty low, and when you walk you can look in anybody's house. But because he looked, this white woman saw him and screamed. Immediately he was arrested and the story was that he was trying to rape the woman. The poor boy was practically lynched by the white folks. The woman finally came to the courts and said that he had just startled her.

Incidents like this just stuck in my mind. I think I was looking for stuff like that. But then again, some of it came close to home.

My brother, for instance, had plowed with two big gray horses from sunup to sundown for the sum total of fifty cents. He was started off at twenty cents and given a raise. The other white guys who were working were making good money. I saw the mistreatment and was determined in my young life that that was not going to happen to me. My kids weren't going to have to suffer in this fashion.

When we had company coming to our house, we kids very seldom got anything to eat, because Mom didn't have enough to feed the company and us kids. So in my home when we wanted to treat our guests and make them welcome, they ate the breast of the chicken and the legs, we ate the heads and the feet.

30

Chapter 3
Introduction
to Kathryn Kuhlman

I wasn't thinking anything Christian in those days. I just wanted to make something of myself. So in Pittsburgh I was making good money, this Jewish gentleman Mr. Harris, was treating me royally, I got a taste of it and I liked it.

Grandma lived in Pittsburgh. She smoked a pipe for 60 years and never thought anything of it. As a result of smoking that pipe, Grandma developed a cough. When she died in January 16, 1974, she had never been in the hospital for any serious sickness. She was healthy. She had in her young life picked 200 pounds of cotton a day, and was just a little slip of a woman. Also, she had given birth to eleven children. A man said to her, "Mother Murphy, you should quit smoking that thing. You are going to fall off of it one of these days." (So you can get an idea of how small she was!). From this cough, she would gag to breathlessness sometimes. The doctors told her if she would quit smoking perhaps the cough would go away. How do you quit a 60-year habit? You just don't put it down right now unless there is another power (God's power) over you.

Christianity in those days didn't mean too much to

me though my sister Timmie Davis, who was living in Pittsburgh at the time was a beautiful Christian person, and to this day moving strong in the Lord.

Little did I know that my grandmother's testimony, her prayers along with my parents' prayers was going to be the turning point in my life.

A white lady came to Grandma's apartment to take her to a service. I thought this was just awful that this *white* person would actually come into a black person's apartment. We never mixed with the white people. We didn't want to.

This white woman came to the apartment and drank tea out of black people's cups. Grandma could care less. I wondered who the lady was. She didn't tell Grandma too much about the meeting, except that she would be blessed by it. Grandma went. You see, we were good Methodists, we didn't go hobnobbing all over the country to all these meetings. But when Grandma stepped across the threshold of this building she was amazed to see nearly 3,000 people inside. It was packed. In those days this group was having two services, and sometimes four, we found out later. When Grandma stepped into this building, nobody prayed for her, but God instantly healed her of that cough, and took that desire for the pipe. Just like that.

My grandmother loved people. You'd expect with all of the things that happened in the south that she would be turned off toward white people. What with Granddad having to disappear like he did. She knew what had happened because he would sneak back but couldn't stay. He would sneak in and sneak out. They didn't like that kind of living. He only lived about four years after that and died. I believe he was just hurt to death.

Through all of this my dad and mother, and grand-mother, (Mother Murphy as she was called) never, never quit loving Jesus, and never quit loving people. I think because they kept loving Jesus, they could love the people—white and black.

When there was a prayer need, they'd call Mother Murphy. She had told me about a white man we had share-cropped for who got deathly sick and dad, mother and grandmother went and prayed for him. He was supposed to die, but the man lived some 20 years after that. This was the kind of prayer warriors they were. This was the kind of belief they had.

Through all the tragedies, through all the hurts, through all the lynchings, through all the misunderstandings of the races, my grandmother hung right in with Jesus. She wasn't an educated woman, but she knew the Bible from cover to cover. She could quote from Genesis through Revelations. She'd say, "Turn to Genesis 6:3," and while you were turning to it she would quote it. She not only had it in her head, but she had it in her heart too. She lived by it. She knew God before she went to the meeting. Can you imagine what she was like when she came away from there! Ridiculous, really.

Grandma became fanatical. If you came to her apartment she would start praying for you. If you smelled wrong, she'd lay hands on you and "zap" you. And she didn't miss me.

My sister had told me something about these meetings before, and so had Grandma, but they didn't tell me too much about all the white people because they didn't feel it was necessary, or else they felt I would refuse to go when asked.

They had been inviting me. "Come on and go,"

they said. But I'd always find some excuse not to go. I always loved my sister Timmie, and, of course, my grandmother. I respected them and I didn't want to be disobedient toward them.

Timmie was well-known and has a beautiful voice. My cousin Mary, Grandmother and Timmie used to sing together in a trio. They were known all over Pennsylvania and other states because their voices were so outstanding, high and beautiful, and had tremendous harmony. This they had learned on the cotton fields down south. They had found the Lord and had a gospel group that traveled all over the country singing.

Grandma, after being delivered of this smoking habit, began to invite me to go with her to the meetings. "You gotta go, you just gotta go to these meetings." They didn't tell me they'd be all white people there. Had I known, I wouldn't have wanted to go. They hadn't told me there would be a couple of thousand people there. But they did say it would be on a Tuesday and that they had asked the people to let me sing. I did a little singing in churches in those days, so I thought it must be all right. And that it must be all black people. Well, if they wanted me to sing . . . . I'll go.

When we arrived it was jam-packed with white folk. They were all grinning—the silliest grins on their faces. The grin or look on their faces seemed to say "We're going to get you." And I thought, *You ain't about to get your hands on me.*

That serivce I sang, "Every Time I Feel the Spirit." I was fresh out of the south and I had that old "down on" beat. We were getting it all together and they were trying to clap. It was then I discovered that white folks couldn't keep a beat. However, we had a great time singing. I sang the same song three or four times and the people gave me a standing ovation. I thought, *these white people are not half bad.* Many of them had come without having supper.

I was under the delusion that all those people had come out to hear me sing. They didn't know anything about me. Here I was trying to outdo myself.

I thought this meeting was for Grandma and Timmie so I should dress up. I put on this super-sharp black suit. I was a cab calloway special. It was a straight suit. I was with the "in" crowd and I wanted everybody to know that. Young people today think they've got some style—why they don't have any style! That suit had every style you could think of in it. The pants were baggy and it was tight . . . so tight I had to pull off my socks to pull the pant legs over my heels. And I thought I was with the "in" crowd! And there I was with my suit and my cab calloway chain. I was "dapped" as the kids say.

I had a bad walk in those days. I wish the readers of this book could see the walk I had. I used to fix my fingers like two six-guns (you had to fix them a certain way behind you), and walk with head up (black folks are proud folks). And, of course, I had my pride. I wanted everyone to know that here was Willie Murphy. I sang my song and when I finished I'd take a little bow, plus my little gazzy walk and sit down.

When I finished this woman came out on the platform. Just the squarest person you ever saw in your life, I thought. She was not with the "in" crowd. I didn't know too much about her. I had only heard her name several times. The kid next to me said, "That's the preacher lady who is going to preach the sermon." Then he told me her name was Miss Kathryn Kuhlman.

Well, I thought, *Who is this? Why, she's going to*

steal the show from me!

When she walked on to the platform all the people stood and applauded and began to praise God. I didn't know what they were doing, but they were making funny sounds. I know now that they were giving glory to God. They weren't so much praising her. They loved her, but her ministry was so dynamic that when she came out she exemplified Jesus to them and so they stood and they praised God together with her. But it bothered me. I thought she was going to steal the show from me. I worked hard for the applause and she didn't do a thing but just walk out and they were all standing and applauding.

Immediately after this kid told me she was a preacher woman, I turned off, bang—right now. Because I was from the south and some of the churches teach there shouldn't be any women preachers. Women should keep silent in the church. And here she is trying to preach to me.

I didn't like the way she walked. I didn't like her talk. I didn't like her voice. I didn't like anything about her. But the amazing thing about her was it didn't make any difference what I felt, or how or what I thought of her. It seemed to hurt her, it meant a lot what she thought of me, and she let me know it. Because even if I was turned off completely, just wam-mo right now. She just sort of turned around and said, "Willie, oh, Willie, we love you." And I just went—Oh, right down to the floor! It just melted me. I had heard that she had something. She possessed something that I didn't. The people who were looking on, the people who were applauding—their smiles—there was just something about those people. They had something I didn't.

I put up a good fight. I tried to pretend I had the

exact same thing they had. And I didn't have it at all.

They didn't ask me if I was a Christian. They didn't ask me what church I belonged to. They just welcomed me. They invited me in. I could see those people loved each other, and they loved Miss Kuhlman. Miss Kuhlman loved them and now she was turning that love unto me.

And yet I couldn't love her. No one's going to suspect me of being a disciple of Christ, not if I had to love that woman. She was a white woman. I didn't want to love her. I didn't hear a word she preached. She preached for two hours.

When the meeting was over the people shook my hand. *These people had something I didn't have.* It was in their handshake. When they shook hands they meant it and you could tell it, you could feel it. (Not the dinky little wet type of handshake).

After the meeting a man by the name of Pop, tall man, about 80, was just beaming with the love of Jesus. He ran after me, his arms outstretched. I didn't know what he was getting ready to do. I'd never been in a meeting like this. He ran after me and actually tried to hug me. Imagine! I wasn't used to hugging men in those days, and especially *white* men. I had my hand outstretched, he just grabbed ahold of my hand and said, "Hello, there brother. God bless you," and shook my hand. I knew he meant it cause when I got my fingers back I had to separate each finger, he had glued them together with that handshake.

And then I began to wonder. I know funny things happen in the south but Mama never told me, and I know I'm Irish because my name is Murphy, but she hadn't told me I had a brother who looked like that fellow. He's not even my cousin, yet he called me "Brother!"

I couldn't understand terminology like brother, sister. This didn't relate to me at all. It should have because my folks were tremendous Christians and I'm sure there was a brother-sister relationship in the Lord in the church, but I'd let myself get away from that. I didn't even want to be connected with it.

So these things didn't mean anything to me when I heard that. As a matter of fact, he turned me off. But I couldn't get away from the fact that he had something that was genuine.

Chapter 4
Born Again

Miss Kuhlman invited me to come back to sing, and I did. She didn't have to use me. I was just a nobody. I'm grateful to her that she loved me enough to invite a little insignificant person like myself to be a part of such a great, fantastic, world-wide ministry.

She said, "Will you come and sing for us again?"

Without realizing it, I said, "Yes." I knew I didn't love her. I knew I didn't love the people, and I think I only did this to please my sister and grandmother.

I went back time and again.

Then she started a choir. She asked those who wanted to be a part of the choir not to miss our own home churches, but when we weren't busy with our own churches if we would to help with the choir. I was asked, "Would you help out in the choir and sing tenor or bass. Can you come and help?" Just to get the applause of the white people, I went. Not because I loved them.

I'm grateful today that I was stupid enough to do it for that reason because it was going to be the thing that was going to change my life later on.

When one is desperate, one does ridiculous things.

Sometimes the Lord lets us get our backs to the wall so that He can get our attention. He was letting this happen to me.

By this time Mary and I had a couple of children. I was working at the Carltonhouse Hotel also. Working two jobs, earning more money now than I had earned in all those years put together up to that point, and yet things weren't going well with us. We were having some debts, actually more debts than we could pay. All kind of things were happening to us and we couldn't quite understand why it took so much cash.

A few years went by and I was working three jobs. I was working at the Carnegie Library as a janitor, at the Carltonhouse Hotel (I quit the job in the clothing store), and took a job as a cement finisher. In spite of all I was doing we couldn't pay our bills.

Many times there had been Christians who had come to help us. Miss Kuhlman too had been one of those who helped us tremendously, and I'm grateful for that.

I was in the choir now, had been for several months, but was not a Christian. I thought I was but wasn't. I had a lot to learn.

The choir rehearsed for several weeks, and we did our first concert with Miss Kuhlman in the Stanbough Auditorium, Youngstown, Ohio.

Miss Kuhlman preached a sermon from the Scripture in First John. When she got to the ninth verse she said, "If we confess, he is faithful and just to forgive us all unrighteousness." And then began preaching about confession. She said that many people go to church. They just go Sunday after Sunday. They are good people but they have never been born again and never have confessed Jesus Christ as Saviour. She pointed out that these people are not aware that they are not Christians. She talked about hatred. She talked about prejudice. She talked about pride.

It seemed everything she read from the Scriptures, everything she talked about had my name in front of it. It was so condemning. I thought my sister and grandmother had written her a fifty-page letter: "This is your life Willie," because it seemed to point me out.

This first concert was packed with people, and when the choir finished we had to scatter throughout the auditorium where we could find places to stand or sit. I went to the balcony because I didn't like Miss Kuhlmans voice. I didn't like her looks. I just was trying to get away from her. She didn't know that.

I have never given my testimony in a Kathryn Kuhlman service, not even to Miss Kuhlman because so many people get born again, and she didn't know too much about me. She had done many acts of kindness for us, but knew very little about my background. Yet, when she preached I was so under conviction.

I thought I was already a Christian. That is the worst thing that can happen to you—for you to think you are something that you are not. I should have known I wasn't a Christian because of all the hatred, all the bitterness, all the pride, all the stubborness, and all the rebellion.

At this time I was rebellious against my own parents (they didn't seem aware of it), to any suggestions they might have offered. I didn't have anything much to do with them. I thought my mother didn't love me any more because I had gotten married and she really didn't want me to marry.

And there were all my prejudices toward the white people.

I had acquired a taste for alcohol too. I thought it was a thing a man should do: smoke, and, of course, be able to drink some liquor. If he couldn't do that he was still a boy. When in high school we found some moonshine. Getting out of high school at our prom, I figured if you are going to be a man then you ought to be pretty near drunk by the time you are 17. For the prom, Mary, my date, and I went out and I bought me a quart of moonshine.

I had my dad's little one-seater Dodge. We went out and I drank about a half quart of that stuff before I realized it was poison. It just about killed me. I didn't know my feet from my head. After taking Mary home I went back to the dorm and all the boys were drinking. We just thought that was the thing to do. It didn't have anything to do with Christianity, it was just a manly thing to do.

That's how I felt now that I was in Kathryn Kuhlman's ministry. I wasn't a member of her staff, I was just singing in the choir. I didn't think anything was wrong with drinking, or smoking, or me having an occasional chick on the side. That was the natural thing to have these kind of things, and yet it was wrong. I know that now. But I allowed myself to believe these things.

God was going to change all of that on that first Sunday when Miss Kuhlman preached that sermon about being born again, about confession to Jesus Christ, about all the pride and hateful things that I was doing, that I had never confessed Jesus, and as she began to point her finger (I used to tell people in my testimony that Kathryn's fingers are not straight, and she had a bad habit of pointing in those days), it would go all the way around the balcony of that auditorium,

42

and somehow or other, she forgot me in the back balcony. And then she'd come back and say, "You in the balcony, up in that balcony, on the first floor in the balcony, you need to be born again. You need to get saved." And her fingers were so long that it seemed they actually reached up to the balcony and they would straighten out when they wiggled on my nose.

I knew she was talking about me. I must have been grumbling and said something out loud because the kid next to me said, "Oh, was she talking about YOU?" It startled me that she would point her finger. I had forgotten about preacher's pointing their finger. It had happened in Jackson Prospect Church in those early days when I first went to the altar. I recalled that that man did the same thing. He pointed a finger and I went to the altar. When Kathryn Kuhlman did that I remembered, clear as a bell, that it had happened in my early life.

Now here I am, this woman pointing her finger again, but this time there was a difference. As she pointed her finger, as she read from the Scriptures, as she preached the Word under the anointing of the Holy Ghost. The Holy Ghost brought that Word to my remembrance and brought what she was speaking to my heart. And I knew for the first time that I was not a born-again believer, that I'd never confessed Jesus. So I found myself instead of running out of that church, because I wanted to get out from in front of that woman pointing at me, I came down with my wife and instead of going out we found ourselves going down to the front where there were perhaps 500 or 600 people going forward to confess Jesus.

There weren't too many blacks going forward. Here I was going to the front, and for the first time with my hands raised up high to heaven. I had never put my hands up in church like that. I didn't think Christians were supposed to.

The churches in the south were a bit different. They believed in shouting when the Holy Ghost fell upon one. It would take six men to hold one person down. Maybe they just got that way so the men could hold them down, I don't know. But it was something going on in those churches in those days. But I thought it was for uneducated people. My determination was when I got to be a man I was determined to get out of a situation like that. I would go to a place where people were quiet . . . where you could walk in and wear a nice suit. So, that's the way we did it. We had found us a good Methodist Church and nobody smiled because if you did the pastor would know you were up to something. So you come in dignified, with no smile on your face, and you sit there. Probably good sermons were preached but you didn't hear too much of what was going on. I found that going to church on Sunday was the best time to sleep. I would sleep for forty-five minutes, or whatever the case might be.

But on this Sunday, I heard this woman preach and it absolutely tore me up on the inside. I saw myself running down to the front of that auditorium, with my hands outstretched and upstretched to heaven—and I didn't believe in that. And I knew they had to be our hands because they were the only four black hands up, my wife's and mine, in that whole crowd. There we were, weeping. And I never cried as a boy. I was taught that men don't cry.

I remember stepping on a nail as a little boy, an old rusty nail, right through the middle part of my foot and it came right through to the top. I hopped home with that board with the old rusty nail sticking in the board on my foot. Mama just grabbed it and pulled it out and put some kerosene on the wound. Then I went back and played. Never cried, you understand—tough!

There were the four of us boys and Dad used to tell us, "Don't fight because if I catch you guys fighting, I'm going to kill you." And when a Methodist preacher tells you he's going to kill you, he meant it. He'd pick up a 97-pound Bible, or something or other, and he'd wear you out. When we wanted to fight, we'd go off in the field and we'd beat each other to a pulp. Then we'd brush ourselves off and come home whistling. Dad never knew we were fighting. The last whipping I got was for fighting. I don't fight my brothers today. We don't even argue because I remember that whipping, and yet I couldn't cry.

One of my brothers was going to make me do something. He was older but I wouldn't do it. He was going to *make me* do it. I was bigger than he and he wasn't going to make me do anything. One word led to another. Before long we'd make the Vietnam war look like child's play. We went to Duke City right now. (Duke City—that's fistville).

We didn't have time to run off into the field, we only made it to the back of the barn. The battle was on. He hit me with an empty bucket he was supposed to use to milk the cow. He picked it up and cowtailed me, right across the head. That's why I don't have any hair today. He knocked all my hair, all my brains out—almost. But he made a mistake and dropped the bucket and let me get my hands on him. And now Dad should have separated us.

It was early in the morning, but he had told us if he ever caught us fighting, he was going to kill us. We

45

wanted to take care of most of that first. That's why he let us fight. I picked up the bucket and went to my brother. We had fought so hard and so long that we couldn't even raise our arms. When we got to this condition, then Dad moved in. He drug us to the front of the old barn. He had been working the horses or mules the day before and left those plow lines hanging over the fence all night. They had acquired a certain amount of dampness, or wet really. Dad took those plow lines and doubled them and laid us down across two old jacks, or two old horses (they were used for remodeling the old barn at the time) and laid us face down.

He said, "Boys, I told you I was going to do something to you if I caught you fighting." And added, "I hate to do it. It's gonna hurt me worse than it hurts you fellows, but I've gotta teach you a lesson." And with this he began to go up one side and down the other. And very calmly said, "Boys, it hurts me worse than it hurts you." I don't know where Dad got that idea. Don't think it didn't hurt! That man whipped the tar out of us. Welts were on my back two months after that. He literally tanned our hide, and yet I couldn't cry.

I couldn't cry, but that Sunday when we ran down to the front of that auditorium, the Holy Spirit had gotten ahold of my heart, and for the first time I wept. I saw that I was sinning and I needed a Saviour. When Miss Kuhlman said "If you confess" that verse leaped into my heart. Also the scripture John 10:10 "The thief comes not, but for to steal, and to kill, . . . but I am come that you might have life and have it more abundantly." Those scriptures stuck in my heart and mind. I knew that I had never confessed Jesus, and

I said, "I am sorry for my sins."

With both hands upstretched I said, "Jesus, I'm sorry for my sins." When I said these words, "Jesus, I'm sorry for my sins. Come into my heart. Make me a new person," it seemed God just didn't have any mercy on me in those moments. It was as though a searchlight went on in my heart and God hung a screen before my face. I was standing there with my eyes closed, crying like a little baby. All I saw was something green and ugly. It seemed the ugliest sight one could ever imagine. This screen had the words: hatred, pride, self-righteousness on it—an ugly green sight, and in my mind I said, "God, who's that? What's that?" And God just let me know that was me. That was *ME!* I had no defense. All I could say to my Lord was, "Lord, forgive me. Please forgive me. Please come into my heart. If what Miss Kuhlman is saying is true that I have never confessed you, I confess you now. Please come into my life."

When I said those words, peace, peace that can only come from Jesus, came in. Something went out of me in those moments that has never come back, and something came in that has never gone out.

I was born again that Sunday. My wife was born again.

Then I went back to my church where everybody was just so quiet, where everything was so decent and in order and dead.

The thing that really convinced me that the Lord had come into my heart at the Kuhlman meeting was when I finished crying I actually had my arms around the neck of a white fellow. For the first time I was hugging a white man and my desire wasn't to choke him.

I knew I had been changed.

I went from there back to my home church. As we were singing some of the dry songs I wanted to share with somebody so badly what had happened to me— about my salvation experience. I must have been moving around making a lot of noise. One of the deacons said to me, "What's the matter with you Willie. You are kinda noisy. What's going on?"

I said, "Man, I've been born again, I've got religion."

He said, "You didn't get it here so be still."

He was a little mad at me for making a little noise around the church.

I had to decide whether I was going to continue to go to that church, or whether I was going to go where I could really be fed, and I made the choice with my wife.

My decision was made on the basis that since I'd been invited to sing in Miss Kuhlman's choir and that I was getting fed the Word there, not that I couldn't have gotten the Word at this other church, it's just that my heart seemed to relate to this ministry of Miss Kuhlman, this is where we would join.

Our kids were born and brought up in that ministry and Sunday school. All came to know Jesus as Saviour there. We had a beautiful relationship in the 18 years of Miss Kuhlman's ministry.

I wasn't a special soloist voice, but I did quite a few solos for the choir and for her when she would call on me at different times. Her favorite song was "Every Time I Feel The Spirit."

Chapter 5
"Mr. Big"

In Miss Kuhlman's ministry there were hundreds and hundreds of people in attendance. She perhaps never met them. I think I might have been one of those people. Even though I was around there for 18 years I never had a chance, and never did I even look for a chance to give a testimony. There would be others who would come in and give great testimonies.

Today, I have the opportunity to speak in many, many denominational churches. God has used the little testimony of my hatred and my deliverance from hatred to salvation to reach the lives of many of my white brothers and sisters.

God can take a little insignificant person and their life and testimony and use them for His glory. We just have to be willing to give it all to God.

I praise God for Miss Kuhlman's ministry, because out of it, I have something that God has given to my family.

Up to the time that I had found the Lord as my Saviour in Miss Kuhlman's ministry, I couldn't tell my wife (not from my heart) that I loved her. I had never told her point blank: "I love you." I couldn't. I didn't think those words should be in our vocabulary. I didn't think anybody loved anyone. God didn't even love us it seemed because *Why do I have to work so hard. Why were there people who were starving?* I would always look for an excuse not to love the Lord. I was looking for a cop-out.

I thought, *Love is just a four-letter word we shouldn't be using.*

Mary knew I loved her because I'd pinch her elbow or something. She knew by that. She could *feel* that I loved her, I told myself. But I couldn't just sit down and look her in the eyes and say, "Honey, I love you." That's how far the devil had gotten me away from God's love. And it wasn't God who did it, I did it.

I knew the Word of God because I was brought up in a Bible-believing home, but I turned away from it. When you turn away from God things like that happen.

Now I was beginning to see the light because I invited Jesus in. He was dealing with my heart along these lines of love. I found myself able to shake hands with white people, and just relate to them on a one-to-one basis. It was so easy. I had to apologize for some mistakes in this area after I was saved. I didn't want to hurt anybody. I loved people now.

I gave my testimony in what was then the *Sun Telegraph* newspaper in Pittsburgh. I worked at the Carltonhouse and one of the editors who came by I knew, and he heard that I'd been born again. He didn't know anything about being born again, but had heard that Willie had a salvation experience. He asked me if I would write my story for the newspaper. I wrote it.

I told everything I knew, and a few things I wasn't sure of. I wrote about being in the Jr. choir of that church and how I didn't have the desire to drink any more, that Jesus was in my heart because I remember being in the choir and after choir rehearsal on Thursdays, all of us guys took off and would go to the Elks to get Pabst Blue Ribbon, get a cool one, because our throats would be so husky, we needed a drink. But now that Jesus was in my heart I lost my desire. I didn't have to go to the Elks anymore. I had completely lost my desire for the taste of alcohol which I had liked so much. I didn't call anybodies name, but all I said was a group in the church I belonged to. The kids knew who I was talking about. I began to get stares from these kids. They all hated me and said, "Why did you write about us in the newspaper?"

God told me that I had done something that I shouldn't have done. I could have given my testimony in a different way that wouldn't have incriminated those kids, but I gave it just the way I felt it. God made me go back and apologize to everyone of those kids. Not for my testimony, but for my stupidity. I've been learning ever since.

I wrote this article, and, of course, it went all over Pittsburgh. As a result I began to get calls to do some testifying in different churches occasionally.

I can't say how much I loved my wife at that point. I knew I loved her because I married her. I must have loved her. We had a couple of children at this time. Until this time I thought a wife was supposed to be a helpmate. She was to be there. She was supposed to do what I told her to do and if not she needed a beating about once a month. Those are the things I thought. I thought she wouldn't be happy unless she had this type of thing. Now I suddenly realized that I had a woman God had given me as my helpmate who loved me.

The first time I met Mary was at Lomax at our high school. We both played basketball. There were a number of girls on campus there. I was a city boy from Montgomery and this was a little country town, Greenville. They thought I was from Montgomery. That's what I said so they believed me. They didn't know I was from Hope Hull, Alabama. I was a preacher's boy, too, so it demanded a certain amount of popularity. All the little girls, a piano player, a young girl who was going after me—that's what I say now, whether she was or not—so I thought I was "Mr.-Know-It-All." I was "Mr. Big" around school and the church.

At this time Mary was going with a big kid. This kid should have been a football player, but was a weight-lifter and had big muscles. I didn't particularly love Mary but I wanted to show this kid that I could get any girl I wanted. So I went after Mary, and she didn't mind either. She didn't know my motives.

I'd smile at Mary, kid around with her and play with her. I knew this weight-lifter didn't like it. Mary wasn't too sure whether she loved him or not. She was going with him some. We were just kids, about 16.

Mary couldn't stand me is what she told me. But I had so many other girls. All of them were sort of just palsy-walzy. I was kind of a popular kind being a new kid in town. So Mary, I think, did the same thing I did because of all the other girls I was palsy-walzy with. Mary thought, *I'll just show him, I'll get him.* I had the same thing in mind where she was concerned.

She was and is very beautiful, a very attractive girl with many talents. She could cook and sew and etc. She has many more talents than that, but those were the things I could see in those days. She made all the outfits for the basketball team at school, and wedding

52

outfits for the people of the community. I thought, *She is popular in this respect so I'll go out with her.*

We almost had a riot among the blacks at my school because the guy Monroe, the big kid, she was going with didn't go to our school. He went to the city school. Mary and I were in a boarding school (Lomax High and Jr. College), theological seminary-type school. This kid came all the way from the city school out two miles in the country to get our girls, I thought. We had a dance one night at our Christian school. Here came Monroe and brought all of his boys (10 or 15) with him. I had asked Mary to this dance.

Mary lived in the city and in order to get back and forth we walked the two miles to take her home after the dance. Monroe was saying, "We'll see who is going to walk Mary home tonight." I said, "Yeah, we're going to see."

I didn't have anyone on my side, just one little helpless skinny kid from the city, and this guy had 15 husky football players with him. You can imagine *who* is going to walk Mary home. But I was determined I wasn't going to be bullied.

About nine o'clock when the dance was over we started to walk her home. Monroe was on one side of her and I was on the other side, and all these big kids (friends of his). They were flashing their knives. I thought I was gonna get it. I was scared but I didn't let them know it. As we were walking along it got really hot and heavy. I thought, *Boy, I've had it now. This guy is gonna get me.*

Monroe must have weighed 100 pounds more than I did. He was about a foot-and-a-half taller it seemed, so I knew he could kill me. When they started to close in on me, all of a sudden, I had about 20 guys from the campus on my side that I didn't know where they came from. (I didn't realize I had so many friends). "Yeah, who's gonna bother Murph. Murph belongs to us and nobody is going to touch him!"

Boy, then I really got big. Talk about the red rooster, I began to "crow."

We were in front of Mary's house, all 35 of us, and we're screaming and shouting, "Who's gonna kiss her good night?"

"Monroe, you kiss her."

And my guys saying, "No, Willie's gonna."

"Let him kiss her."

"You kiss her, Willie."

Her mother came out about this time and said, "Mary, come on in."

So none of us got to kiss her.

That showed me something and showed Mary something. Mary had to make a choice now—who was going to go with her. Fortunately, I won out because after that we started to see a lot of each other.

I was going to her house on Sunday because I was a hungry boy always, and her mother would cook the best cake and the best chicken. I'd go over on other days and have me a quick dinner and then Mary and I'd get to talk for a while. This went on for two years.

Then it was time for me to graduate. Mary was a year behind me in school and I thought, *I'm going on, I've got a scholarship to go to college and what about my chick?* The good Lord fixed that because Mary and I were able to get married in July of that year that I graduated in June.

We had a great relationship, and had a lot of things in common. I loved being with her parents. I loved her but I couldn't tell her that. It dawned on me that I really did dig this chick, she's all right. We were just having a happy time.

After I quit my job at Goodyear Tire and Recapping to leave for Pittsburgh she decided she would stay home while I go and get a good job and then send for her. There wasn't enough money for both of us to go.

I prided myself in the fact that my dad had the biggest (and only) Methodist Church in Greenville and was popular now. I was proud that I was coming north to Pittsburgh. It was hard for Jesus to really get to me through that pride. But praise His name, He broke through it all.

Mary was Baptist and quit her church when we married and joined the Methodist Church. We were so far from being Christians. We weren't bad but we weren't good either.

After meeting the Lord as a personal Saviour seems as if nothing was going right.

I wasn't used to living high, and now I'm in a choir that's predominately white, with people who had far more than what I had. So I had to have new clothes. I was going to be going to Youngstown (which is about 75 miles from where we lived in Pittsburgh) every Sunday. I had to have money in my pocket; consequently, I, instead of paying the bills, kept the money to buy and do things and got far, far in debt.

One thing after another was just going wrong. I know now the reason why God let me go through some of these things: so that I can help other young people and couples who have the same problems.

During the first three or four years that we were in Miss Kuhlman's ministry, Mary was busy having children. And I was busy trying to be the big guy.

We didn't have a car so I had to hitch rides with

some of the people in the choir and was gone every Sunday. Every Sunday in the choir, on Fridays at the choir rehearsal, and on Saturday at youth meetings. I was very active. I got to the place where because I wanted to shine, I wanted to be like the white people, I think I lost sight of my place as a husband. Now I desired to have things like the white people had. In order to do that I had to be almost alone. I got rid of hate and picked up pride.

I left Mary home so that I could have enough money to eat where the whites ate; to do the things they did: to be able to say, "Hey, come on, I'll pay for this." Mary made a sacrifice to let me go and she stayed home to raise the children. This went on for several years. I would be in church and remember she was staying home so much.

I got so wrapped up in what I was doing that I couldn't stay home with her when I should have been. It got to the place where at times Mary just didn't want me to go anywhere. But I was the man and if I wanted to go I went.

After a while I found that it wasn't Jesus that I was seeking more of, it was just to be in that big choir, it was just to get the applause of the people. It was just to be around the white folks that I hated so much and now I loved. It wasn't Jesus for me at all. I found myself getting in trouble all the time because of my attitude.

In the meetings the Holy Spirit would be so strong, so anointed, that I'd become convicted in almost every service. I'd say, "Lord, forgive me," but the next week it'd be the same thing over and over. This went on for years.

It's amazing how long you can go in a rut like

that, but I did.

I knew I loved Mary, but somehow or other, we were drifting farther and farther apart. We'd have heavy arguments and I couldn't see it at the time, but it was because I was neglecting her. She needed my love, she needed my attention. She needed me to be with her. If we were going to go to church, we needed to be together. I couldn't see it. I even lied to be in the choir. The choir folk would say, "Hey, bring Mary." I'd say she didn't want to come. I wanted to build myself up. It was a pride thing. It was a selfish thing I had acquired.

Some might say I wasn't born again. I knew Jesus. There would be times when I would be so strong in the Lord that I felt I could actually see Him and touch Him, and yet, there'd be other times when I was so in my selfish state that I felt that He had left me and would never return. I knew that I knew Jesus and nobody would ever make me doubt that. I just allowed the flesh to get in the way. We all can do that, if we are not daily dying to self.

In the meantime, I acquired a lot of bad habits. I wanted to make myself appear to be so big in the sight of these white people that I lied about my clothes. I would borrow clothes to wear from my brothers so that I can look as nice as the rest of them, and letting folk think that we had money and things to build myself, to make myself something that I really wasn't.

And yet folk around me didn't know that. They didn't know what I was feeling inside. They just thought, *Hey, man, this is a great kid.*

Chapter 6
Being What I Wasn't

I became a tyrant to my own family.

My sister and my grandmother knew this, but yet inside it was still a turmoil even though I had been born again.

At the time I had been born again I was completely satisfied. A couple of years went by and I found myself almost in the same state as I was before I was born again. There was something missing on the inside. And yet I knew Jesus. There's been a time when I'd feel the Lord so heavy when Miss Kuhlman would be preaching. She'd turn to the choir and say, "Oh, Jesus, bless them." Sometimes almost ninty-nine percent of the choir would just fold over, and if I made up that one hundred percent, there would be only one person who didn't budge to the moving of the Holy Spirit because I was rigid. I was a man and nobody was going to push me over. I wasn't gonna fall out like these kids. It was ridiculous I thought. They were fanatics.

That went on for a long time before I was able to receive God's anointing in my heart. Before I could receive it, God had to do something with my spirit. He had to really teach me some lessons.

Miss Kuhlman preached the Bible faithfully, week-in week-out, and I learned tremendous truths, but unfortunately, I didn't apply it. It was in my heart but I didn't use it.

The Word of God doesn't mean anything unless we apply it to our lives, and I wasn't applying it at all. I had set a goal. I had said I was going to do certain things. I was going to amount to something, and I did everything I could to become someone important. I'd walk over heads to get to the top. I had to make the top. If I had to use people to do it, I would do it and God was going to show me that I couldn't do it that way.

The Lord lets you go so long and then He'll pull the rug from under you, and you'll find yourself out there dangling and you'll be held up by the devil. And God was going to show me this.

While working for this Jewish man Mr. Harris, he made me his head stock man in his clothing store. I felt I was a big man. Here I'd been janitoring, and doing all these other little odd jobs, mopping, and what have you. Now I'm the head stock man, receiving all the merchandise, writing it up and I thought *Oh, man, this is great!*

Before I was born again, probably it was because I didn't know the Lord, but greed got in. The Jewish man paid me good, better than he was paying almost anyone else. Even better than some of the salesmen.

Because of wanting to do so much, because of wanting to be better than the white folks, this greed took ahold of me and I began to steal from this man. Not steal merchandise in the sense of taking it home. For example, I began to sell these things to truck drivers—winter jackets or shoes—at a very low rate just so I could earn some money. I'd sell to enough of them that they would supply several other truck drivers.

I thought there was nothing wrong with this. My alibi was that I said the Jewish man was cheating these people with a high price so I might as well make a little money too, he's not going to miss it. The Lord showed and convicted me of this greed. I wanted to tell Mr. Harris so bad what I had done, but he died suddenly. I never got a chance to repent to him, but I repented to the Lord of the things I had done in those early days.

This greed was in me. I wasn't delivered of it even though I asked God to forgive me of it. I didn't ask Him to take this thing away from me. It was something of the flesh and anytime I wanted to I could rebuke it, get rid of it, but I didn't.

Consequently, when I got saved some of that stuff was stuck with me on the inside, because in order to be like the white folks, or like these big people in the choir, in the ministry, I would use the same tactics. It might not be stealing, but it could have been lying, or some other things, just so that I could get to the top. It was like painting a rosy picture of myself when it was just the opposite. I'm telling people I had a good job, making a lot of money when in essence I was broke. It was that type of thing, and God had to deal with my heart concerning these things.

I have to watch it even today. The Spirit is willing but the flesh is weak. The flesh will say, "You know you're hungry, don't you?" That's the flesh speaking to the Spirit. I have the power of spirit to say, "Be quiet, wait till after the service." But if I don't, and say, "Willie, yeah, you're hungry," I'll probably leave in the middle of the service and go to the coffee shop and get a hot dog or something, and I didn't learn what God was saying in the meeting.

I didn't know how to use my authority as a Christian in those days, but I'm learning.

This very thing has caused a problem, not only in my life, but many Christians who have fallen, who are weak and don't know how to use the authority that God has given us and so fall into temptation. In doing this, there are other Christians who are weak in the same way, and will be condemning toward others. They'll just absolutely condemn others to death, to the point where they feel they can never repent. They can never get repentance of any sin because they've fallen once, and God had to show me in that area. A Christian would fall and I'd say, "Well, look at them, I'd never do anything like that," and would add, "they are lost."

Be careful when you say those things because there comes a time when you'll be caught up in the same situation that you condemned someone else for. God used such a situation to teach me some lessons.

In those early days with my family I was really trying to be more than I was. I found myself getting in all kinds of fixes.

We had bought a house. We couldn't pay the taxes so the house got behind in taxes, and it was all because of my stupidity and disobedience. Yet I was a Christian.

We had bought a car. It was repossessed because I couldn't pay the monthly payments sometimes. I'd try to borrow money—no way, because my credit was so bad.

The things that I was involved in a Christian just shouldn't be involved in.

My debts were bad. My credit was bad. Everything

61

about me was bad, but when I went to church at Kathryn Kuhlman's on Sunday, it looked good to the people. At least I thought so. I tried to make it look that way and I was getting deeper and deeper in money troubles.

God just let me go and go, but He was going to deal with me concerning this.

Finally, my wife said, "Honey, we've got to do something. We can't go on the way we're going. We just can't make it this way. I don't understand you. I don't understand why you do some of the things you do."

At the time she didn't realize that I had some habits I had acquired that I wasn't even sure of myself. I'd want things and instead of telling her the truth about it, I'd take part of the paycheck and buy what I wanted and lie about it. This started when I began to sell stuff from Mr. Harris' store—to use money for my own good, so I'd have money in my hand. I wanted always to have money in my pocket. I never wanted to be broke again. In order to do that I had to sell on the side, steal stuff to sell. This just carried right on through because I didn't get it taken care of when I was born again.

One day Mary said, "You are drinking, and, of course, you stopped that, and you stopped a lot of other things. There's something in you I don't understand. I just don't know who you are. We're supposed to be Christians but things are not going well with us at all."

She was referring to my tactics like instead of buying a little Volkswagon-type car, I always wanted to get the big Buick or the big Cadillac, and it takes a lot of money when you're not working. One should have what one can afford. But I didn't see it that way.

I had to have what I couldn't afford.

Taking a trip was really out of the question, but we'd take a trip and I wouldn't pay the bills. I just wanted to have a lot of money in my pocket.

This went on and on. God was going to deal with me now. He was getting a little tired and a little upset with me. The reason for this may have been my grandmother.

Grandmother had been praying that God would save *every member* of her family *before* He took her home to glory. God was going to honor my grandmother's prayer.

When Grandma had this healing experience I'm sure God filled her with the Holy Spirit. She might not have even known what happened to her but when she'd run out of words while praying under the anointing at times, it would sound as if she were singing and was using the words of the Holy Spirit. I'd hear her down in the little apartment and she'd be before the Lord travailing, praying that God would get a hold of all the members of her family. I thought she was a fanatic, or she had flipped. And that we were going to have to haul her off to the "big house" some place.

Grandma had eleven children and they are all living today but one. This is the beautiful thing about it— Christians who love Jesus, who dedicate themselves to the Lord can live a long time. She really didn't know how old she was, but according to the Bible record she had passed the age of 96 before she died.

She was always praying, and said to me one day, "Willie, you really need to let the Lord get ahold of you. God wants to use you in the ministry. I was with your mama before you were born and we prayed that God would let you be the minister because the others seemingly just wasn't cut out for it. And I know God has called you. I've got on my knees and I've been praying for months that God's going to save you and going to put you in the ministry."

I didn't want to hear that. I just put down the whole deal. *I didn't, I don't want it. I've got an education.* I thought I had it all, I knew everything. I knew that preachers didn't make any money . . . . and yet Grandma was making it like a prophecy saying that the Lord had shown her that I was going to be a minister, and going to be preaching to people by the multitudes. I was going to be persecuted, she told me.

This I couldn't believe because I couldn't believe I'd even be preaching. This reminded me of when I was a little boy. Some of us little kids would talk about how we hated white people because of some incident, and we'd say how we hated them for it. The kids then were kidding me about being a preacher's boy.

I realized I hated white people because of some events early in my life. Like the time a white man smacked me across the head. I thought he was right but I became aware of the hatred.

At one time my brother got hit because he said something back to a white man. He was right my brother, that is. The man accused him of something he didn't do and he said to the man, "I didn't do it." And when he said this, of course, the man smacked him good.

I thought my dad was going to shoot this man. He didn't care who was black or white. My dad was outspoken. He told this man that if something else happened like this, "You tell me, don't you go hitting none of my children." The man respected my dad.

Another incident I'm reminded of happened to my

brother who was next older than I. The one I got in a fight with. He went to the Korean War and when he came back he got married and moved to Montgomery into a new apartment.

All the black people had an apartment section built just for them. They had to pay their rent in one general office connected with this building.

My brother was taught to respect the older people. One day he went to pay his mother-in-law's rent and said to the manager, "I come to pay Mrs. so and so's rent."

The man said, "She's not Mrs. to me, she's Cora."

My brother said, "She may be Cora to you but she's my mother-in-law and she's Mrs. to me."

And with this the man called him nigger, and "You get out of here. I don't want that rent. I'll never take it. Don't you ever come back here again, I'll kill you."

He had been in the war and wasn't about to take this. But because of the upbringing he left. He never could go back to that office.

When he told me of this incident it helped to build up a hatred for white people, with him just telling me how this man had treated him. It made me angry.

At another time a man told a joke and it made me really mad.

He said these two black guys (I can laugh now but I couldn't then) were bootlegging back and forth across the line back in the State of Alabama, and along with it stealing chickens and some pigs.

This one night the police had stopped these fellows and told them that they shouldn't come through town speeding, and they had a tail light out, and that they should fix that tail light.

The third night in a row the same cop stopped

them. He said, "I thought I told you guys to fix that light, and quit speeding through here."

Of course, he said they were half high. They said, "Well, we forgot, we just forgot."

The officer looked in the back seat. (They had stolen a hog.) They had the hog laying down but they set him up in the back seat and this boy took off his hat and put it on the hog.

The officer said, "Who is this nigger guy back here. What's you name, nigger?"

The hog, of course, can't speak so the officer took out his blackjack and hit the hog across the head, and the hog said, "Oink."

He said, "You should have said that the first time."

To me this was an off-colored joke and made me fuming mad.

The rest of the story was that the officer went back to his buddy that day at the Police Headquarters and said, "I stopped three boys and I was going to arrest them, but one of the boys they had with them was named 'Oink,' he was so ugly I felt sorry for him and I let him go."

I left the south because I wanted to make a better way for myself. I blamed the whole south for the things that were done to black people. But when I came north I found that the north had just as many problems.

While working for Tremble Construction Company in Greensburgh, Pennsylvania, on a telephone building my brother who was foreman, or strawboss, as we called them, ran into some problems. Many whites were working on this job.

One white man said, "No black nigger from Alabama is ever going to boss over me."

My brother was kind of a hothead. He wanted to

66

pick up a two-by-four and just about kill the man.

The things that were happening in the south were also taking place in the north.

There were restaurants that we tried to go into, we were told: "We don't serve blacks here."

One day while going toward Erie, Pennsylvania, and having driven all day I was really hungry. We stopped at a restaurant, and this lady said, "We don't serve Negros here."

Of course, I was up tight. I said, "Well, I don't want to eat any Negros, I didn't come in here looking for Negros."

The manager thought I was trying to be funny. But we still didn't get served.

As I grew older this hatred got bigger and bigger, and I didn't express it. I didn't come right out like the kids do it today . . . if they hate you they'd just say, "Man, I hate you." And not only will they tell you that they'll go do something about it.

But I wasn't that type. I wasn't that violent type. I just tried to not have anything to do with the white people.

Even in Miss Kuhlman's ministry it was hard for me to relate to white people. They tried to relate to me, and I put up a fuss, but inside I was aching. *I didn't want to be around them.* Even today I have to watch myself because I rejected for so long.

Also, there's a lot of mistrust. A person may say, "Hey, I really love you," and then you find a knife in your back the next minute. This happened many times before I became a Christian. So you can imagine how it feels if it happened to you after you became a Christian.

I just rebelled in every way I could think of not wanting to love, having an outgoing love toward people

67

of other races. I wanted to be equal to them in every way.

While in Miss Kuhlman's ministry I allowed myself to build up this thing about being something I really wasn't. It would have been almost better if I hadn't become a Christian than to build up something within myself or allow the people to think something about me that really wasn't so.

Of these many lies I've repented of. I've gone to God many times, and to many of the people, and repented. Unfortunately, to some I haven't been able to go. Some of the things just crash back.

Everytime something comes up I'll say, "Lord, how could I have done that. Forgive me." I believe it was because I was born again but not Spirit-filled that many of these things happened. Even when you're Spirit-filled it takes a lot of committment—like 100 percent. It's rededication over and over and over.

I rededicated so much I forgot that I was rededicating. I went overboard—back and forth to the front of the altar saying, "I'm sorry, I repent of this." I believe God heard me. It was sad that I had to continue to do that. And I still have to.

When we come to God we think we are perfect right now, but we know that we're not, and so He's provided a way that we can come to Him and tell Him that we're sorry and He hears us, that's the beautiful thing about it.

In this going back and forth to the altar I found that many of my friends were doing the same thing. I thought I was alone.

Chapter 7
Something Lacking

I allowed myself the pleasure of starting freely now to love people.

If we are going to love somebody Jesus said that we were to love as the Father loved him. That we would do so was His prayer—that the body of Christ would learn to love each other just as He loved the Father and the Father loved him. We haven't gotten to that point yet. I know I haven't, and I want to.

I found I was freer in my expression, or in my love toward the people, the more they loved me, and perhaps the more they would help me because I wanted to get to be popular. I wasn't including my wife in this.

Finally, in working I acquired a car. With this I could take my family to church. The Lord had let that happen because it was a big change in my life. We'd pack a lunch on Sunday and leave at 7:30 in the morning. We would drive 75 miles to be at the church by 9:30 so I could be ready for choir rehearsal by 10, because we went on with performance at 10:30. We enjoyed driving the 75 miles.

My life took on more changes. I began to see Jesus. I began to love the people, not falsely now. I began to appreciate my family more. Many beautiful things began happening.

However, I got in another rut just going to church every Sunday, singing three songs and going back home. Then getting up on Monday morning and going to work. That just went on and on. I thought there was still something lacking. I wanted more of Jesus even though I had rededicated, recommitted my life and everything. There was still something lacking.

We weren't paying tithes at that time, but we gave liberally to the church. The car and gas cost for our free gratus travel those 10 years was several thousand dollars.

I began to get hungrier for the deeper things of the Lord. What I was seeking for was the fullness of God's Spirit.

I was in a rut. I was tired of going to church every Sunday. I went because it was something to do. There had to be more than this to a Christian's life.

Ten years passed after my conversion before I met Dr. Ray Charles Jarman. I met him when he gave his testimony at Miss Kuhlman's ministry and told how God had saved him after having preached for 70 years. I was so impressed by him. He told how a second experience had come into his life.

I'd heard about these second experiences. We call it "baptism in the Holy Ghost," but I thought it was for holiness people or Holy Rollers. We used to live next door to a holiness church. I thought those people were all crazy. They jumped up, they shouted, they walked across the pews, I was told. I didn't want to be one of such a fanatical group. I didn't want to be a part of that. Those who were baptized in the Holy Ghost, all they talked about was the Holy Ghost. So I knew that the word *Holy Ghost* related to those fanatical people.

70

Also, someone had told me that the reason they didn't want to get mixed up with those holiness people was because they actually fall down, or are *slain in the spirit* they called it. One girl said while they were rolling on the floor some guy leaned over and bit this other fellow on the leg, so I thought, *Man, I don't want to get caught up in that group, that's a silly bunch.*

I was hungry for more of Jesus, and when Dr. Jarman began to relate that there is a second experience that Christians can have and all you have to do to be a candidate is to be born again, I wanted this. I thought, *born again and yet when Kathryn turns around to the choir and says, "Jesus bless them" half the choir falls over, and sometimes almost all of them, and yet, I'm the only one who for years remains standing, and I was dry!*

Miss Kuhlman allowed Mr. Jarman to take 130 of the choir kids on Sunday to the Gold Room in the Stanboug Auditorium and explain the baptism in the Holy Ghost. Out of curiosity I went. Mary wasn't there that particular Sunday. I had invited some kids to come to the house after the service that Sunday. We were going to drive back to Pittsburgh, go by the house and have dinner.

Mary had fixed a beautiful soul dinner: blackeyed peas and baby lima beans mixed together, potatoes, barbecued pork chops, fried chicken and cornbread! And when we all got there nobody was hungry! She was mad because we were all happy. We were all smiling. Something had taken place on the inside and she had missed it because she stayed home to cook.

We tried to explain to her that this experience is called "being filled with the Holy Ghost, or baptized in the Holy Ghost," that it's a gift that God gives, and when you receive this gift, it makes you so happy and

71

gives you so much *more love* and *power* that you actually smile more and you want to love people more. That all one needs to be filled is to be born again. And that this filling with power helped one to be an effective witness. That mainly is what it's for—to be a witness.

When Mr. Jarman had explained at the meeting about being a witness, I knew that I wasn't much of a witness. I knew of all those sore spots and weak spots in my life—the greed was there, and like when I found myself wanting to steal. Those spots were there even though I was born again, and I knew that if I was going to conquer them I had to have more power.

Mr. Jarman had also said "I won't pray for anyone here unless you are sure that you want God to do more in your life. If you're afraid of this and you are a curiosity-seeker, and you don't want to be a part of this, before we start to pray I want that you leave the room."

That day 103 of the kids stayed in that upper room. Mr. Jarman gave us some Scripture and then prayed a general prayer. Without exception, everyone received the fullness of God's Spirit in that room that Sunday.

Up to that point I had never been "slain in the Spirit." Whenever Miss Kuhlman prayed I'd stand there rigid. I wasn't going to get knocked over.

I was convinced in that room that day that it was real.

Barbara Coleman, one of the girls, began to sing with the most melodious voice I've ever heard. It echoed to the seventh heaven! I knew it had to be some power greater than Barbara's. It had to be something more precious than what Barbara had. She has a beautiful voice, but nothing like this. I found out later she was "singing in the Spirit."

72

As Barbara was singing the whole choir seemed to be caught up in this. Before long they began to fall like flies all over that room. I too was so caught up, and it was so beautiful, I let myself go. I began to say, "Oh, Lord, fill me, baptize me, whatever. I need it."

When I came to I was stretched out like a lizard in the sand. Stretched out on the floor with my hands outstretched and I was saying, "Ava, Ava, Ava." I knew I was communicating with the Lord. The Lord was right there. I knew I was being filled with God's Spirit.

Dr. Jarman laid hands on no one, maybe a few just next to him.

Most of the 103 people in the room that day are out in ministries today. That filling they got did a beautiful work in their lives.

Little did I know that that was going to be the beginning of something beautiful in my life, and, of course, my family.

Right after that, the Lord began to daily speak to me.

When I got filled it was beautiful. All the language I had was "Ah, Ah, Ah." But I knew I had the Holy Spirit in me, and He was speaking through me.

This new happiness in me created a problem because now the scriptures were more alive to me. Everything about God's Word was more alive. Even the choir was better.

Mary had missed out on it and she got jealous of what God had done in my life. She began to think things, making accusations that weren't so at all. She was seeing something in me that she didn't know anything about. She was seeing more love.

We Christians loved each other before this happened, but it was deeper now. You'd hug anyone you saw. If they were Christians you just wanted to say, "Jesus loves you, and I love you too." We Christians had hugged each other occasionally, but it was nothing like now since being filled with the Spirit. It was like being filled again with love, or born again. It was that love I wanted. I wanted to reach out to people without having any fear. Now, all of a sudden, it happened. I could love a man, a woman without thinking and saying, "I love you."

My wife saw this and said, "These guys are crazy."

She thought we were getting weird: guys hugging guys every time they see each other. It was bad enough to have guys hugging guys, but when guys get to hugging women too, look out, boy, that's dangerous! And it is if it's taken out of context. But when it is done in the name of Jesus, and it's the Holy Spirit upon you it's really all right. If in the Spirit it is pure.

Because Mary wasn't filled with the Spirit she got hostile, even towards her own church. It got to the place she didn't want to go every Sunday. Then she didn't want me to go.

I wanted to go out now and minister, I was turned on. Everytime I got invited to go somewhere, I was ready to go.

We had a group singing (Ultratones), and were going out and ministering to people. People were being saved. It was beautiful.

Mary became jealous of all these things that were happening. She knew something was taking place but she didn't know what. I didn't know enough about it to explain to her. We told her all we knew but it wasn't enough.

A number of years went by. The Charismatic Movement had erupted by now. I didn't know anything about charismatics. All I knew is that God was pouring out His Spirit—something good was going on.

I began to meet the leaders from across the country right in Pittsburgh.

We started going to Full Gospel meetings. It was at one of these meetings the language God had given me became more fluent. I wasn't satisfied with the language I had. Though it was good I wanted more. Some Full Gospel people laid hands on me and prayed that God would make my language grow and make it more fluent, and the gift He'd given me would become so evident in my life that I could be a witness with vigor and vitality, with much love and much boldness.

As they were praying the Holy Ghost came upon me, and I received a fluent language. It was beautiful. I just enjoyed it so much. Every time you pray and ask God for more He gives you more—you just go from glory to glory to glory.

Little did I realize all that my mother and dad, sister, and grandmother had been praying for me that God would make a minister out of me.

God had to do a lot of work in me.

I was going through so many changes. That's why I had to sit under Miss Kuhlman's ministry for 18 years, to get all that teaching. She preached 20 years ago the things that I hear preached today. God had put all this in my heart so that when He did get me ready for His ministry, I'd have some knowledge of the Word and I'd be able to share it.

As I began to grow in the Lord, Miss Kuhlman was a little worried or concerned that her choir flock was going out. She didn't know too much about what they were doing or where they were going, and one could understand that.

I understood it. She was just saying, "If you are going to go, I want to know where you are going, and if you are going to go in the name of this ministry I want to know. And if you go and you're not going in the name of this ministry, don't include this ministry's name anywhere because I can't be responsible." I respected that.

I knew that I was going to go into the full ministry because God had been calling me.

I had a very good job with the Sunshine Biscuit Company. Just one job now. Things were just going beautiful and everything was just great financially.

At least, almost.

Chapter 8
Call to the Ministry

I was filled with the Spirit but I didn't know much about the Spirit and I didn't really think too much about the Word other than what I had heard preached and what I put in my heart.

When you are ignorant of so many things in God's word you make mistakes. You make mistakes even when you know a lot about God's Word. I had made my share of mistakes.

Because of the baptism of the Holy Spirit and because of the love I felt for people, sometimes this love was misused, mistakenly. Not on my part always but on parts of others. Because I can love people I was taken advantage of.

I knew when the Lord called me into the ministry. He simply said to me as I was reading the Word one day I was to sell out, I was to take up my cross. I was to leave mother, father, wife, children, everything for his cause and He would take care of my needs and my family, and that He would not separate us. I was to sell out everything for *HIM*. I was to love *HIM* above everything else. He showed me this in the Word so clearly. I was reading in Luke 14 when this occurred.

I was reading in the verses about where Jesus said unless you're willing to leave mother, father . . . and as I was reading He said would I be His disciple and take up my cross and follow Him? He was seemingly saying to me, "I want you for the ministry, to be a disciple, and I want you to share my Word, whether it be in Word or song, I want you." And I knew it was the Lord. I knew it.

In the meantime I was having these problems with Mary because I couldn't relate to her. She didn't understand why I could feel like I did, how I could love people.

She'd question me: "How can you love people like that?"

I began to meet people, all kind, male or female, and because I loved the Lord so much and I wanted to help people and wanted to love them, I began to relate to these people and I could minister to them. I've seen many get saved and some get filled with the Spirit. I knew that God's call was upon my life.

I got hired on this new job with Sunshine Biscuit Company and got in the management field. I began to doubt my call. I thought the Lord needed me on that Sunshine Biscuit job and that this call that I had to go preach—wasn't from the Lord. It could have been from the devil, I thought. I used this excuse for two years.

I prided myself with that position with Sunshine Biscuit Company, and in doing so turned away from the call of God.

I had eight prophecies in eight different places from people who didn't know each other who prophesied prophecy over me in meetings. It was almost word for word. It wasn't something I didn't know, it was something the Lord had already said to me. It was actually confirmation. When the prophecies came I knew it was the Lord speaking to me.

But in spite of all that I fought the call. I rebelled against the call of God and went ahead trying to make something of the job with Sunshine Biscuit. It was a good job. The people I worked with were fantastic people, but the Lord had said to me, "I want you to resign and go into the full ministry."

I argued, "Lord, I can't do it because there's not enough money out there."

And as a result of my outgoing spirit I began to try to find people who could relate to me. Christians need to be careful not to put people up on pedestals because when we do we make a God of them and we can be let down. God allowed that to happen to me so I would keep my eyes on Jesus.

All the friends I had acquired in those several years after being saved and filled with the Spirit became closer and closer to me. I just began to relate to them. Most of them weren't filled with the Spirit, though they were saved. What they saw in me was Jesus, that at least was what I wanted them to see, and most of them did. They saw Jesus and they began to say "We see Jesus in you. Oh, it's Jesus shining through you." I allowed what they were saying.

This credit they were giving to me went to my head. The Lord allowed it because I had turned from what He had called me to do; doing my own thing, making my own sunshine, making a big name for myself. I allowed the devil to get into my life because of it.

I had made some friends, beautiful people. I loved them with all my heart. They loved me. We developed a tremendous relationship between families—Mary, and my kids and their kids. Everything was going along just great, really great. I allowed the flesh to enter into this situation.

Because of the moving of the Holy Spirit in my life He allows us to have so much so freely.

I loved my friends, and they became closer to me than members of my own family. But I allowed the flesh to move in, and it was because someone said something about one of the people. One of my friends did something that I hadn't noticed before, but all of a sudden, because I took my eyes for a second off of Jesus, I allowed the flesh to move in. Now this one incident was going to change the whole situation.

Because I was rebellious in being obedient to the Lord when he had told me He wanted me to resign my job, because it was my job that allowed me to have lots of time that I could move around and be with my friends. If I had been ministering perhaps some of these things that I allowed myself to get involved in, I wouldn't have had the opportunity.

I ought to have known that when God speaks to us and we hear His voice that it's important to follow Him because He knows the future.

Because I was disobedient I let myself go to my friends rather than to go to God. I began to look to my friends. I began to depend on them when they would say, "You're great. We love you."

In this type of atmosphere I wasn't careful enough, or I wasn't with the Lord enough and I didn't know enough about the Holy Spirit to know that I was being swept in—not by my friends but by the devil.

This went on for months. I would leave my job and go see my friends. My wife didn't know about it. She couldn't stand most of my friends because they were filled with the Spirit. Many of the people whom I was seeing, however, were not filled with the Spirit. Perhaps if they had been there would have been some roadblocks.

I don't blame my friends for what happened in my life. I am totally responsible for the things that took place.

The Lord also shared with me during this time that when I went into the ministry that I was to move from my beautiful surroundings in Pittsburgh where I'd lived for almost 20 years. He wanted me to take my family and move. He didn't tell me where. He just said, "I want you in the ministry and you will move."

At this time I was in a couple of charismatic meetings as song leader. I met some beautiful teachers of the charismatic move from California. Some of these men were invited to dinner at our house. Dick Mills and his wife prophecied over Mary and I, and told us the same thing that God had already told me two years prior—that I would be in the full-time ministry—that the Lord would pave the way and support us in every detail.

Dick also told Mary that she wasn't filled with the Spirit. How he knew that only the Lord could have told him. And with this he said, "If you want to be filled I will pray with you now and God will fill you."

Mary was hungry and said, "Yes, pray with me." Needless to say, she was filled.

Dick also gave some prophecy from the Scripture to the seven members of our family, and all seven of the prophecies have come true.

The first of these was that God would lead me into the ministry away from my job into another state, and that God would give me the finances to travel. In less than one year this came to pass.

He also said that we would receive $50 in 20 love gifts. We not only received 20, we received some 30, but the amount was exactly what he had prophecied.

He also said we would be given a home wherever we moved to because we were obedient to God. It meant that we had to be obedient to receive God's promises.

I said, "I know the Lord has called me," but I left it there and a few months passed.

After Dick prayed with Mary she received the baptism and became a glowing, beautiful person. She got to the place where she actually trusted me. And when she trusted me, I became even weaker. She even trusted all of our friends which she could never do before.

I kept on with my job trying to make a go of it. As a result I met a girl. She was one of the dear friends we had. I used her as an escape, deciding that God hadn't called me into the ministry after all.

I decided I would leave Mary and go away with this young girl. We would leave town. We both planned it.

We left and when we got away we both *knew* it was wrong. We were both wrong.

Mary didn't know what was happening to me. This girl's parents didn't know we were gone. We felt it was so bad what we had done, but reasoned that Mary wouldn't want me back, and neither would her folks want her back. She was of another race.

Here I was, hating people of other races, and yet I found myself thinking that I was deeply in love with someone of another race! It was the devil leading us. He didn't want me in the ministry. Satan didn't want the thousands of people to come to know Jesus to whom I would be preaching God's Word.

I wish to God I could have known this before. In those days I needed a Spirit-filled brother to talk to. But I didn't have enough trust to go to one of my brothers. And after this happened I felt I didn't dare go to anyone, so I tried to keep this a secret.

When we both found out that we had made a mistake, we wanted to go home. Both of her parents agreed, and my wife agreed it had happened and we would tell no one about it . . . just keep it to ourselves. We were going to pray and ask God to forgive us of it and forget it.

It was all agreed, and we went back home. Everything was supposedly going great with both families. We had several family meetings together—families again.

I went to her parent's home and asked them to forgive me. They agreed.

I had done this after I had decided that God had called me. I felt I had "blown" it. I had messed up God's plan. I began to ask His forgiveness. I bargained with God: *If You'll help me get out of this situation, and forgive both of us, I will go into the ministry full time.*

Chapter 9
The Mistake

We sold our home in Pittsburgh and decided to move west. We didn't talk with anybody about the situation. I had already been to California several times. It was from here I'd written this girl several letters. I signed my name to them. I loved her.

I wanted to get out of obeying the call of God. I wanted to go my way. I needed someone to be with me, and I knew my wife wouldn't have agreed to it so I turned to the other girl.

Now this was all over. Forgiven and forgotten. I thought!

I didn't ask for those letters back. I let this family keep them.

Everything was going along smoothly. No problems, God has restored me to the ministry. I had resigned my job with Sunshine Biscuit Company.

Things were happening for us in California. People were getting saved. I saw individuals getting filled with the Spirit, and on many occasions healings, so we knew that God had gotten glory out of all this that had happened. There were two years of beautiful happenings.

Now, after all this time, the family that had said

they had forgiven me turned against me and became very bitter. I can't say I blame them. What I had allowed the devil to do in my life and what I had done with their daughter by taking her away, I can understand that they would be upset. They were furious.

What I couldn't understand was that after two years of saying everything was all right, and working together in many, many drug ministries with this family, that now all of a sudden they could turn and do what they did.

One of the letters I had written while I was in this sin with this girl, this precious mother of this daughter kept, began to make copies of this letter and erased her daughter's name, just leaving my signature, explaining how I loved this girl (the letters that I wrote were gussy), and how I wanted to be with her, and how I wasn't getting along with my wife (which was true). I was thinking of leaving my wife even if I didn't go with this girl because I was being rebellious to the Lord.

This letter got into the hands of my Christian brothers who did not try to understand. They said, "You lied to us."

When I first came into the ministry and they asked me to sing, they never asked me anything but just to come and sing. This I did. They didn't ask me anything about my personal life. At the time I was working for Sunshine and wasn't ministering full time. I had lived in adultery, but was forgiven, and now for two years had ministered with these brothers and had been very straight, very honest.

But when they got this letter from this mother they believed every word of it. Because I hadn't told them for two years prior to that, now I was condemned.

85

It was a rough period.

One of my Christian brothers whom I loved very much was a man I had worked with for two years. I told him of the experiences and said since we were going to be working together he should know about this. The mother knew we were working together and began to call him. And when we were in the area where she lived she tried to see him and tell him things. Things that he already knew.

One day the Lord told me, after working two years with this man, that he had called me into the full-time ministry and that I was only doing part of it. He had told me to be alone and do preaching and singing, but because I was disobedient He had cut our finances. It wasn't as it ought to be. We weren't getting enough from the meetings sometimes to pay our air fare.

One day I said to my Christian brother that I thought the Lord had called me into the ministry and that perhaps I was going to have to go into the full ministry myself, and perhaps he should do the same. He became very violent and said that he needed me with him and that I couldn't work without him. He knew too much about me and if I decided to quit working with him, then he could destroy my ministry.

I didn't know that a man of God would do such a low thing. He didn't deliberately do it I'm sure, but he was hurt and I could understand why he would be hurt. We worked so well together and we could still be doing it.

I decided when he told me this that I'd better stay with him because he did know enough about me, and one word from him and I'm dead. So I stayed with him. But God had strongly impressed me that He wanted me full time.

86

We were ministering together in a place called Spring of Living Waters, and this man had a violent heart attack. It was so severe he passed out and we had to rush him to the hospital. The attack was so massive the doctors told him he would be bedfast for at least six months, and that he wouldn't be able to work for a year or more.

After this he said, "Willie, I feel that you ought to cancel our meetings and you better find some meetings that you can do."

I did exactly that. I called all the places where we were engaged to come and cancelled. Then I wrote places and called people I knew and told them I was free to come and minister. I booked myself for almost a year. The Lord opened the doors.

In the meantime, there was a world convention coming up for which I had been asked to do some singing, and I went. I took the news about this gentleman being sick. The Full Gospel people prayed for him—5,000 people joined hands. This man was miraculously touched by the power of God.

God raised him off of the sickbed within three weeks. The fourth week he was at home, and by the fifth week was ready to go again.

He called all of the places where he had asked me to cancel and rescheduled meetings without telling me. Then he called me and said, "Willie, I'm ready to go, and we can start next week."

I told him I couldn't because I had meetings scheduled that I was going to do. I had committed myself and there was just no way I could cancel these meetings now and go with him. However, I agreed I would work with him whenever I could, and with that he became very violent.

The meeting which we were to do was a regional meeting. He passed the word that "I don't know what Willie's doing any more," to one of the men where he had booked us both. The man had billed me as coming. My Christian brother said to this man, "I don't know if I can trust Willie. He has a past of running around with whites, getting involved with white women."

There had only been *one* woman I was involved with. "He has a past and I'm not sure but what he may be involved now," he said. The other man picked this up and passed it on to a leading man in that state where I was to do a meeting by myself. This man called and said, "Willie, I hear you're running around the country with white women, and for this reason we can't have you come and minister."

A series of events like this happened. The word began to spread.

Then the girl's mother began to spread the letter around saying, "Hey, this is the kind of guy you've got coming." And with this I began to get a number of cancellations from around the country.

But God through all of this, even as I would get a cancellation, He would open a door where I could minister so I would never be left without a ministry. Through all of this God honored.

I became very discouraged when this began to happen.

One of the biggest meetings that followed I was going to do alone, was a meeting where there would be at least five or six thousand people, brothers and sisters of the Lord, and I so wanted to be there. My wife had planned to go, we were going to have a great time in the Lord together, but when I got a call saying I couldn't come—I was cancelled, I thought my world was over. *I'm ruined,* I thought.

I began to complain to my wife. She became very angry and said, "I told you, you can't trust white people anyway." We thought everything had ended for us. God had not honored us, had not forgiven us. I felt now as David felt in that time. I thought I had done something so low that I could not be forgiven of it even though I had gone to God and had asked Him to forgive me, had asked Him to vindicate himself in my life in any way He saw fit.

I'm very grateful today that it happened because I know now how to talk to others who've had similar situations. I can counsel with them and love them, and express to them that I know God hears and answers.

When this door was shut for this beautiful meeting that I had so wanted to go to, God opened another door and it was a better one because in doing so a call came the next day saying that there had been provisions made for us to make a world tour. So instead of just going to a one-state meeting, God let us visit 18 continents on this world tour. On one of the stops we made we had a chance to sing before two million people via television in Hong Kong, so I know that God was in it.

My Spirit became so grieved for I had been so discouraged before this call for I had decided to quit the ministry.

I remember the first time I thought I was so called of God. My first call was to go to Omaha, Nebraska, to a Presbyterian Church where the Holy Spirit had fallen, and where people were being healed and saved. I didn't know anything about what the Holy Spirit was doing other than He had touched my life. In going into this church where the Holy Spirit was already moving, I thought *I* was bringing in some great ministry there and

89

here I was just moving in on a situation that had already developed.

So when I went in and preached and sang and God honored the Word the people got saved and filled, and there were some that were healed. I came home to my wife an oracle of God.

I told her, "Oh, honey, everything is just great. You're looking at an oracle of God!"

She said to me, "Oracle, would you take out the rubbish."

So I just knew things were all right.

Shortly after that I got this call saying, "Hey, you've fallen from grace. You've messed up and you are cancelled."

I became discouraged at one little bit of persecution. I had forgotten that I was to be willing to bear all things . . . love bears all things . . . love even when one is persecuted . . . and love doesn't return persecution. God had to teach me that.

I had yet to learn to love my brothers and sisters even when I'm being persecuted by them. I was to love them in spite of themselves, and I wanted to be loved the same way.

I knew that what the men said in some cases they could have been sued for. It was true, in my past, but they didn't give me the opportunity to repent of it. They didn't even ask if I had repented of it. They didn't ask me, "How was I doing." They didn't say, "I'll pray for you." They just said, in so many words, "You're condemned, you've messed up."

The Bible says we should go to the brother in error, and if he won't listen to go back taking some brothers along. None of these things happened in my case, unfortunately.

Before making the world tour I was so discouraged I told my wife I'd never, never sing another song, never preach, I was through with it. One day I took my *Living Bible* and went to the ocean at a private boardwalk area in the residential section. I sat on the edge of that thing and with my feet over the water I began to bawl before the Lord and said, "Lord, did you really call me into the ministry? Did you really forgive me of that sin I committed? It was a bad sin and I know that and I've asked you to forgive me. Your Word tells me that if I come to you and ask forgiveness you would forgive. Lord, I don't think I've been forgiven. If I have been how can those who say they love me, my brothers who are very close to me, whom I've worked with for two years, how can they now condemn me? They know now I have repented. I've told them so. How can they condemn me without even any love at all—not even any more communication. How can they do it, Lord? If you really called me, how can you let this happen?"

For about six hours I travailed before the Lord. I begged Him. I beat on the boardwalk. I cried. I got no answer seemingly from my Lord. He never heard me. He never talked back to me—nothing.

When I went on that boardwalk, I was the only person out there. After some hours I did look back and there were a couple of ladies sitting under a big umbrella. They weren't paying me any attention, and I didn't pay them any.

I kept praying. I kept asking God to show me. I told Him I would not leave that boardwalk until He revealed himself to me. I knew He didn't have to reveal himself to me, but bless His name, He did! In his grace and mercy and love He heard my cries.

All of a sudden a gentle breeze began to blow. My

Bible that was laying there—open—I hadn't looked at it for four or five hours—casually the pages began to turn and stop at Isaiah 43. The very first verse the Lord was saying that He had called me. My Spirit began to just burn on the inside, and I knew that it was the Lord speaking to me (even though He was talking to those Israelites). He said, "I called thee." And then suddenly the pages began to flip some more, to the forty-ninth chapter and again it said, "I have called thee." Then again it flipped to Isaiah chapter 43. There I read, "I have called thee by thy name . . . when thou walkest through the fire thou shalt not be burned; when thou goest through the waters, I will be with thee; and through the rivers, they shall not overflow thee. I'm the Lord that called thee." When I read these verses something inside of me leaped and I knew it was the Holy Ghost.

I screamed, I cried, "Thank you, Lord." I jumped off the boardwalk down in the ocean. I jumped back up. I clapped my hands. When I looked back those two ladies were really trucking. They were getting out of the boardwalk, but I could care less. I was having a good time. I was having a good time in my Jesus. I knew that the Lord had heard my prayer.

I had called on God in my time of trouble and He heard me. He answered my prayer and delivered me. He told me now to glorify Him.

From that point on the Lord has honored his promise to me that He gave that "I have called thee by thy name. I will be with thee."

The Lord has done that. There is no malice in my heart. There's no unforgiving spirit in me for I love everyone—even those who felt the need to persecute me. I want these brothers and sisters to know that I love them and pray for them daily. I pray that they too can love me as I love them. And that "we might be one" as Jesus prayed.

Six years have gone by. Still a few of those letters are being circulated. There are still those who say that because of my past that they can't trust me. These are my brothers and sisters. God doesn't want us to go through life with guilt of any kind against a brother or sister.

Mary had said, "How could you let yourself go. How could you get so involved when you loved God and He was using you. How could you let yourself fall in love with another woman when you had a wife and children?"

I'm an affectionate person, a person who required or needed lots of love. Not that I didn't get it from Mary, my wife. She's the most loving person I know. She did everything she could to please me, to make a good home for me, and she did it quite well.

When the flesh gets in the way, the flesh is really weak. Deep in my nature I was the type who liked to flirt with the girls; liked to have a good time even before I became a Christian. I loved to be around the girls. I loved the chicks who were playing basketball. I loved to have them make a fuss over me. After I became a Christian I didn't kill those things. I didn't let them die. They were there and given an opportunity, the devil knew when he can't use anything else he'd use the flesh when my eyes got off of Jesus.

I was such good friends with these people who trusted me (that's why I could understand when they became bitter). It probably just suddenly dawned on them after two years what a mean thing, what a bad thing, what a terrible thing it was that I allowed to happen.

One day I woke up and here I am in the middle of a situation that was too big for me to handle. And needless to say sorry—sure, we both were sorry. I can imagine how David felt. He had planned what he was going to do. He looked out of the window one day as he had perhaps for years. He didn't just all of a sudden go to the window and look out for the first time, he had been looking out of that window for years. Now this is the gospel of Willie Murphy: *he'd been looking out of that window.*

But all of a sudden when he looked out this particular day, he saw a woman, and that woman was beautiful, and I have to believe that his mind wasn't on the things of the Lord the day he looked out. He became lustful toward her and he desired her so he asked her to come over. And, of course, he had relations with her. (I wish I could speak to David. You see, I'd like some questions answered too.) I'd like to know why such a thing could have happened to him. It happened so quickly to me that I was shocked when it happened.

I woke up one day and found that I felt a strange sensation for this girl. That's a trick of the devil. I know that now. Had this been a few years before that when I became a Christian, I wouldn't have come within ten feet of that woman. I wouldn't have had anything to do with her because I didn't like white people. Now I knew the Spirit of the Lord was in me. I loved Jesus and I loved everyone. I loved her parents. I loved all the other folks I knew. And I find myself loving her more than I did myself. We planned to leave together. We knew it was wrong, but we were still duped by the devil. We allowed ourselves to go through with it. We wanted to be alone, and with our lustful desire toward each other we went through with our plans. We were wrong, and had sinned.

All is not lost. We could go to God. We can be forgiven. "I write unto you, that ye sin not. And if any man sin, we have an advocate with the Father, Jesus Christ the righteous" (I John 2:1).

It is so easy today that so many people in the great move of God will be caught up, great men of God, in the lust for the flesh.

I pray that God can teach us, all of us, and show us this danger.

Everyone of us has a sex drive, and we have to realize that the love of God is fine. That true love that God gives us when He fills us with the Spirit is just beautiful, but if we go beyond that love then it's a fleshy love and we fall into the trap of Satan.

I entertained the thought, I put the thought into practice, and it became a sin. God tells us that it is a sin. It's no sin to be tempted. The sin is when I yielded to the temptation.

I know that my sin has been forgiven. My sins are under God's blood. I have no doubt about that. The difficulty lies in the area that though my friends know Jesus has forgiven me, they can't forgive me. They still can't trust me. They can't believe that God can wash me clean. They can believe for themselves that they be washed clean, but they don't believe that it can happen to another person.

God would like for us to understand that if we go to him, He forgives and he forgets. And He wants us to forgive. I must be willing to forgive the persons whom I've hurt—and those who have hurt me—that is by the grace of God, by the mercies of God, by the love

95

of God and by the power of God. And I want this same forgiveness from others. I can't demand it, but I sure would love to have it. I would love for us to be able to come together and say, "Hey, listen, you know I blew it. Let's pick up the pieces from this point. Let's get turned back unto the Lord. Let's go on from this point. Let's not let this happen again." Maybe one of these days we'll get that way as a body.

All that has happened to me has helped me to grow deeper in the things of the Lord. It has made me love my brothers and understand them more and be less dependent on them, and more dependent on God.

Chapter 10
Sandra,
Quincelia and Marion

I used to think the minute you are born again and after being filled with the Spirit of the Lord that you automatically become a super-boy, super-person, and that your problems were no longer.

Oh, how wrong I was!

The things that happened in my life are not there so that people can look at my dirty linens, but that someone might see that looking at the weaknesses and problems that I had and that it might be something that will help them to grow, and not to make the same mistakes.

Mary and I have a family. We have five children.

God has blessed us with beautiful, beautiful kids.

I'm a grandpapa, the youngest (probably) in America!

We have the cutest little granddaughter you've ever seen!

Our children have personalities, each one of them different. We couldn't treat any of them the same. There was always something about each of them that was different and we had to deal with them just a little bit differently. And we found as we dealt with our children, that God deals with us individually the same way.

God dealt with me in my weakness and my problems in one way. Then I found others of my friends, or my brothers and sisters who had problems that weren't exactly like mine. That God had to deal with them in an individual basis. Where I have fallen into an adulterous thing, there have been others of my friends who've never committed adultery, but they have either stolen or were gamblers, or have hated their mothers or their fathers, or others. But God in his tender mercy dealt with each of us in His own way and forgave us.

Now He's teaching us also how to help our own family.

We have our four daughters and a son, our youngest being a little girl, Sandra. That's my baby. I just love that kid. Of course, I love them all, but there's something about Sandra. She's so timid, we call her absent-minded. Tell her to bring a glass of water and she'll come back with a glass of pop.

We never really had too much of a problem with our oldest daughter, Quincy. She "hates" us because we named her that, but it was the best name we could find at the time.

Quincelia Murphy. Quincy was just a great kid. Has a smart head on her. She finished with honors and could have gone into college. She had letters from Washington—they wanted her to go into a special business training thing. She did take some training in business. Applied for a job with the government, and was hired almost immediately. Today, after being with this company for six years, Quincy now is one of the office managers for the State of Pennsylvania.

When she was 14, she went into the store with five

girls from her school. She had never stolen anything.

I used to tell the kids, "You can't do wrong and get by. The minute you do something that's not right you'll be caught."

Evidentally I got through to her because when she went into the store the other kids stole stuff and all got away. She was the only one who got caught with a pair of gloves.

The manager was furious because these kids had been coming into the store, picking up stuff and walking out.

Quincy was so embarrassed she wouldn't tell the store manager where she lived or who her parents were.

The manager was so mad he called the Juvenile Court.

About three hours passed. Mary and I became worried, wondering what had happened to Quincy and how come she wasn't home from school. We called around to some of our friends. Finally one of her friends said, "Last time I saw Quincy she was in Treassure Island."

This store was several blocks out of the way coming home from school so she would have to go out of her way to go there.

The only thing I could do was to go back to the last place where she had been seen.

It was near 10 o'clock in the evening. I asked the manager, "Have you seen a little girl around?"

He said, "What's her name?"

I said, "Her name's Quincelia Murphy."

"I had her arrested. She was in here stealing out of my store."

I just knew that my kid couldn't steal! Why, I'd already told them if they'd steal they'd get caught, so I knew she wouldn't be in the store stealing. I got a little infuriated with the man and said, "What do you mean, my daughter's in here stealing and you had her arrested."

He replied, "She's in Juvenile Court right now because I had to take the little monster there for stealing, in fact, I'd try to kill half of them if I could catch them."

I got very indignant.

Since then I had to go back and apologize to him because he was only trying to protect what was rightfully his, and the kids were stealing.

I called the Juvenile Court. Sure enough QUINCY was locked up. They had tried to find out from her who her parents were and where they lived so they could contact us. She was so embarrassed that she gave them a fictitious name.

When I called they said, "Yes, we have her here."

To get her released she had to be placed in our custody.

Quincy tried to explain, "Mom, they caught me, and I hadn't planned to walk out with the stuff, and all the other girls got away." She gave a whole bunch of explanations.

From that day till this, Quincy has never stolen anything.

That experience taught her a lesson. But more than that—teaching her a lesson—she was brought up to know that to steal was wrong and that as a Christian it was wrong, and that she feared God more than she feared us.

She told the Lord she was sorry.

I didn't scold her too much but tried to show her how wrong she was.

We taught our children the fear of God. I don't mean they thought of God sitting up there with a cat-of-nine-tails waiting to spank you every time you step out of line, but a God who loves, a God who loves so much that He's got so much to give that you don't need to steal. That He loves you and you don't have to steal, and even when you steal you can still go to Him and get forgiveness. Quincy learned through this experience that she could go to God and He would forgive her.

Another daughter, Marion, 19, and married, was so different from Quincy.

She thought she was the cutest girl in the family. She won a runner up in a group of ten at the Orange high school beauty contest in competition with 25 or more girls. She was the only black girl so she sort of prided herself in being one of the ten finalists.

It went to her head.

She was a powerful, kind of arrogant little girl. We knew that. We warned her but she wouldn't listen.

We let her think she was good looking (and she is!). She could do anything . . . she could be president of the United States if she wanted to! We failed to tell her that she had to have humility along with all this: she had to have love, she had to have understanding, and she had to be honest.

Consequently, when she got out of high school she and her boyfriend were going to go away on vacation. She decided one night at 2 o'clock in the morning that she was just going to go along with him without telling us. She had never been away from home. She had never done anything like that.

I came in from Nebraska to the Los Angeles International Airport, arriving about 2 o'clock in the morning. My wife met me at the airport, and normally the kids would be with her. They enjoyed coming down, taking the ride to meet dad. But this night they decided to stay home. Mary said the kids were a little tired so they stayed in bed.

When we got home at 3 a.m. I went in to check on them. I wanted to give them a big smooch a-rue, as I always did. Sandra was there and I gave her a big hug. I felt in the other bed for Marion. There was no Marion.

I saw her bed was still made up, it hadn't even been slept in. I asked, "Where's Marion?"

"I don't know," said Sandra. "She was here."

I thought she might be with our daughter Beverly who was pregnant at the time. She might have been sick and Marion went to stay with her.

Since Beverly's husband was a policeman and was on duty at the time, I called to find out if Marion was with Beverly. "No, Marion isn't here," she said.

So, I waited.

I was very much concerned. At 6 o'clock we still hadn't heard anything from Marion. By 9 a.m. I was beside myself. She'd never done anything like this before. What's wrong? Was she kidnapped?

Her mother had a little car and the little car was gone so I thought Marion must have the car.

I checked the closet for her clothes—all of her clothes were there. She must not have taken anything but what she had on her back, and her purse and no money. She couldn't have had more than $1 in her purse so I knew she couldn't be too far with no money and that old car of her mother's.

Noon came. Still no word.

I got in my car to check around with the kids

where she'd gone to school. Nobody had seen her. It never dawned on me to think about the fellow she was dating.

David had come around several times. When Beverly got married, he was in the wedding. He seemed like a cool kid—didn't say much.

Marion would get dressed up when he came and he would say to her, "Why are you getting so dressed. Why don't you just put on some jeans like I have on?" I didn't like that in him. I'd think he would want his girl friend looking as nice as she possible could. But he seemingly wanted her to be sort of a tramp type. No care. "Don't comb your hair, it's not necessary."

He didn't have any get-up-and-go about himself. I didn't care for that about David. I hadn't questioned or said anything too much to her or to him about this. However, I did caution her to be a little careful—to make sure she knew who David is, and not to just be led by some kid. To know what she was doing.

She had a pretty good head on her so we trusted her. It never dawned on me that my daughter, only 17, would pick up with some kid and leave home without even the slightest warning. She had been going out with him occasionally. There didn't seem to be any problem.

About 2 o'clock in the afternoon I thought we'd better call David's mother and see if David knew where Marion had gone.

Mary called and talked to his mother. "No, we haven't seen her. David's not home. David has gone to Texas on his vacation to visit his grandparents," she said.

Now I was really worried.

I thought I'd better go to the police. I hated to go to the police. I didn't want some kind of a bad story

103

coming out, but I was desperate so I went to the Orange Police Department.

They knew about Marion because she was one of the winners in the Miss Orange contest, and she'd been with the firemen and with the Police Department on the big parades, and had done modeling for the big department stores, and other activities in the community. I showed them Marion's picture. They knew her immediately and said, "We know her, and she's missing?"

I said, "Yes."

"Well," they said, "she has to be missing 12 hours before we can do anything."

I said, "She's been missing longer than that."

They immediately began a process of notifying all their units, and other units in the area.

At 6 o'clock in the evening, still no word.

I called David's mother again and asked her, "Do you honestly know that David went alone?"

She hadn't heard anything so didn't really know that they weren't together, and surely David wouldn't do a thing like that.

When she said this, I thought, *My Marion wouldn't do a thing like that either!*

It was then the Lord seemed to let me know that those two kids were together. Instead of becoming concerned for their lives, or what was happening to them, I began to get mad. Really, really, really mad. I wasn't willing to let Marion do something wrong and believe that God could help her. I wanted to kill that guy.

I was Spirit-filled and supposed to be filled with the love of God, supposed to be filled with wisdom, supposed to be understanding, but in those hours it seems as though I lost all of that because I was so mad at both of them. I was furious to think that they could do this to me.

Here I am an evangelist trying to help other young people, not realizing that in my own life some of the same things were happening.

Momentarily I forgot that we have to be willing to let someone make mistakes, and let *God* correct them. I forgot my kids are free moral agents, and are subject to the same errors as anyone else.

I was so upset I forgot we have to be forgiving and understanding and help our kids when they make mistakes. God was using this experience to teach me this.

I went back to the Police Department and told them that I believed the two kids were together. David was 19, and my daughter 17. In the State of California that meant she was a minor. David was of age and if he was picked up with her he would be arrested for contributing to delinquency of a minor. That would be another strike against him. They had my wife's car, which at this time now could be reported stolen, so David was going to have to account for a stolen car. Since he was with a minor and if they were going to Texas and going across the state line with a minor he was in more trouble.

The police said I could get them on five or ten counts.

They put out an all-points bulletin throughout America, Mexico, and Canada that if they were found they were to be arrested on the spot, because of a stolen car, contributing to a minor, etc.

A day went by and we still hadn't heard anything so I called David's mother again. I don't know why I kept doing that, but somehow or other I felt that it had a bearing on the case.

This time when I called she said that the kids were in Texas together. (I think she knew it all the time but she didn't want to alarm us). She said, "There's nothing wrong with the kids going away on weekends."

We didn't teach our kids to run away with fellows on weekends alone, unchaperoned; we just didn't think it was right.

I asked her to give me the telephone number in Texas where they could be reached. She hesitated.

Finally, I persuaded her to give it because if she didn't I was going to have the Police Department there pick them up and arrest them.

I called this number and David's grandfather answered. He said, "Yes, they're here. The kids have gone fishing. Don't worry about them. They are together in our extra room."

Why would he have them staying together! That just burned me up more.

I asked to have Marion come to the phone.

Finally, when she came to the phone she said, "Hi, Dad."

I said, "Marion, (I didn't even say 'Hi') what in the world's going on with you? What's wrong with you?"

She said, "Oh, David was going away on a vacation and I didn't want him to go by himself so I decided to go with him."

She knew that I was opposed to this, but she was so far away she figures I couldn't hurt her. The next few words I said to her, she got the idea that I didn't like it too much.

I told her to take the next plane home as soon as we hung up.

She said, "He's only going to be here two weeks. I'll just stay with him and I'll come on back when he comes."

I was so up tight I took a plane.

Her mother in the meantime called Marion and said, "Your Dad is coming, meet him at the airport."

I got to the Midland, Odessa Airport and called Mary when I arrived. She said I was to wait there because Marion was going to pick me up.

These kids were fugitives, they were criminals. I noticed in the airport an all-points bulletin of these two kids. I'd given pictures to the Police Department in Orange so they had both the kids' pictures.

I called the Police Department that I had found the kids, that they could drop the charges.

When the policeman saw me in the airport he immediately said, "You can't go out and get them, you don't look like you're ready to greet them with open arms. We won't let you do it. We're going to go with you."

I insisted that I'd pick them up. By this time I had waited about two hours for Marion. I was really mad.

I knew the address. I said, "I'm going to get her."

The officer said, "No, I'll take you out."

Whereupon we got in his car and we were going to go out to pick these kids up, and when we pulled out of the airport driveway, who should be pulling in but these two kids. They didn't know that I was coming in an officer's car to pick them up. The officer turned around and followed them back into the airport.

When they parked the car and had gone I moved the car (I had an extra set of keys) so they couldn't find it if they tried to run away.

I was thinking the worst thoughts about my own daughter. I couldn't think anything decent about her at all. I thought if she'd open her mouth I was going to smack her really good in front of the officer. In fact, I was going to tell her to stay there, I didn't want her anymore. I was going to tell her she wasn't even my daughter. And, if that kid David said anything to me, he wasn't going to see any love of God in me at all. I was going to pull his head out at the neck and throw it to the moon.

The officer knew that I was very mad. He waited till I moved the car and then I walked into the airport behind them.

They were standing in the middle of the airport looking all around. I heard David say as I walked up behind them, "I told you that he wasn't here. He's so mad that he's left."

I tapped them both on the shoulder at the same time, and when they turned around they were startled. Marion said, "Oh, Daddy, you're here."

I said, "Yeah, where else are you expecting me to be." I was going to start to really let my venom out. I was ready to get that kid. She knew it.

Something happened on the inside of me at that moment when our eyes met. All the hatred, all the things I'd thought somehow or other vanished, and sweetness came in my spirit, something beautiful, something peaceful.

My daughter was saved and I knew it. All I could say to her, rather than smack her on the face or say something hard to her was, "Marion, you know I love you."

I began to weep and we embraced each other.

I discovered that my daughter meant more to me than all the bad thoughts that I had, even if she had committed every sin in the book, I loved Marion and

and Marion knew it.

And instead of smacking David, or pulling his head off and throwing it to the moon, I shook his hand and said, "Hey, fellow, you know, you guys have really blown it, you've made a mistake. This is not the right thing. This is not the way you should have done this. This is wrong."

I turned from David then and said to Marion, "Marion, you took your mother's car," and explained the charges against them.

I'm grateful to God that He gave me a heart full of love for my own daughter, and for a fellow that wasn't even in my family. A fellow who wasn't even a Christian.

All I could do was embrace Marion. But I did tell her that she had taken the car and it was wrong for her to do it.

I was going to take the car back to California, and was going to leave them in the airport together to discuss the thing they had done, and that Marion was free to go home. It was her home. We loved her. We wanted her back, and we'd help them if they wanted to get married. What they had done was wrong and we hadn't agreed to it. If she wanted to go back home and talk about it, make some plans, fine. Whatever she wanted to do, but in twenty minutes I was going to start that car and I was going home to California.

This is not like me at all. I would normally have taken her bodily to the car, threw her in and locked the doors. And if David would have said anything I think I would have pulled both his arms out, and yet this didn't occur to me at all.

I went to the car and sat there twenty minutes. Marion came and said, "Dad, we talked it over and I want to go home."

I was so happy I jumped out and grabbed her and hugged her.

We put David in the back seat and took him back to his grandparents and left.

Those 20 hours I spent alone with my daughter. I learned something about myself and about my daughter that I hadn't known, even though I'd lived with her for 17 years.

God showed me that I hadn't given her the attention I should have given her. That she had a lot of questions she needed answered. Many times she had tried to talk to me, but I was too busy, or said, "ask your mother."

The Lord in His mercy convicted me, and I had to confess to Marion that I was sorry for not having loved her as I ought, and been the dad to her that I should have been for so long. I asked her to forgive me. She asked me to forgive her.

God showed me something else in my daughter.

I was in a pair of old jeans. I was so mad I didn't care how I looked.

I only had seven dollars in my pocket when I left home, and a Mobil credit card. It was nearly 1,700 miles back to California.

We couldn't find a Mobil station open between Midland and El Paso so I had to take $4 of that seven and buy gas to get from this section of Texas to El Paso.

When we got to El Paso it was near 9:30 in the evening. I noticed that our tank was just about empty and our stomachs were just absolutely dry and empty. I hadn't had anything to eat all day long.

We took $2 of the three that we had left and bought some hamburgers.

We had $1 left. We started out. We still hadn't found a Mobil station and didn't know if we were going to find one open this late on a Sunday night. We thought the best thing to do would be to go back to El Paso to a family, the Lewises, whom I had met a year ago.

I recalled that they had a church meeting that was meeting in the YMCA in El Paso. It was almost 10 o'clock at night and the meeting would be over, we thought. Maybe we could stay there.

When we arrived we discovered that Rev. Bob Lewis, a Southern Baptist preacher, had a meeting going on right then with an attendance of 300-400. Every one was praising God with singing in the Spirit and their hands upraised. We sat in the back so that we wouldn't be recognized (me in jeans).

In the midst of that beautiful worship and praising of God, my Spirit began to leap on the inside.

The Spirit of the Lord touched Rev. Bob Lewis. Even with his eyes closed he knew that Marion and I had come in the room. He said, "Willie Murphy just walked in." I turned white. I didn't expect that. "Come on up Willie and sing for us," he said.

I was in no shape to sing. I had just had a tremendous experience with my daughter. I was incognito and I just had never appeared before an audience like that in my whole life, but that was the real me and evidentally the Spirit of the Lord directed Bob to do that.

When I went to the platform and tried to open my mouth to sing, nothing came out. Nothing. I was so full I just couldn't, I couldn't open my mouth.

I had $1 in my pocket. We were still over 1,200 miles from home. Nobody knew anything about why I was there. Nobody knew why Marion and I were alone,

111

or why I was incognito the way I was, shabbily dressed the way I was. No one knew anything, but those people ministered to us.

Those were real brothers and sisters of the Lord. They ministered and ministered to us. While I was standing there trying to sing, the people were praying. I could sense their praying. I was trying to open my mouth and nothing seemingly came out.

All of a sudden I noticed that my daughter had slipped to my side and she began to say something, making a confession—what she had done—not in detail, but just that how God had pulled us together for these many hours. How we had related to each other and now the beautiful thing He's done for us. She asked the congregation to pray her, and for us as a family.

I had to make a confession publicly to my daughter before those people, and with this God so beautifully touched our hearts.

My daughter began to sing a little chorus written by Debbie Kerner: "Jesus, Jesus, He died, he rose and he lives, and he lives. Because He lives we live, and because we live we recognize that He is King of kings and that He's Lord of lords. He's a forgiving God."

We sang "Hallelujah," and by the time we got to the last verse of that little chorus there was such a high praise God began to bring the people forward. The problems we were having in our own life related to the people.

The people came forward. Some of them were getting saved all over again. Some of them were being healed. Some of them were slain in the Spirit even as we worshipped and ministered there together in the name of Jesus.

We'd never had an experience like that before,

nor have I had an experience like that since.

Some of those people I had only met once, some of them I hadn't seen for two years. They came and shook hands and told us how much they loved us. Each of these gentlemen as they shook my hand, placed in it a number of bills.

When we left that night we had close to $200. No one knew our situation, but God knew.

Because of our learning to love each other, to forgive each other, to be not only father and daughter, but to be brother and sister in the Lord, and to have the love for the other parts of our family members, God's family, God honored that and showed us something.

Needless to say, those last 1,200 miles going home were the greatest.

Before I left California her mother had said, "I'll have her bags packed, I don't want that girl in my house. Her bags will be out on the porch. She can take them or leave them if she wants to. I don't want anything to do with her, she's given us a bad name!"

When we got home and I opened the door, who do you think ran out and grabbed Marion and said, "Oh, Marion, I'm glad you are home! I love you."?

God taught us that in each of our children He is showing us even ourselves. God has shown us that we have to love each other. That we have to be forgiving, and to give each person an opportunity to be wrong, to be human, to be a person, to be an individual. We are to love them, and help them.

David and Marion are husband and wife today, and we love them.

Chapter 11
Beverly and Irwin

The other girls think I love Beverly more than I do the rest of them, but it isn't so. I love them all the same.

I was more protective of Beverly because she was so gullible. She didn't think anybody would do her any wrong, or any harm, and especially the guys. She was just a soft touch to the boys because she trusted everybody.

Beverly was having some serious problems at 15 or 16, and I had to keep an eye on her all the time. I just couldn't trust her out of my sight.

In one sense she was gullible because she just didn't understand, and in another sense she just didn't care. She was a loving girl and would do anything asked. She was so helpful to her mother.

She had a different personality than any of the others. I didn't want her to get hurt. Beverly got into some serious problems.

I was in Tacoma, Washington, when I got a call from her mother saying, "You're going to have to come home, Beverly's get a serious problem."

We were willing to accept whatever Beverly's problems were and work with her in it and love her in it. God worked it out to the point where what we thought was such a big problem, wasn't even there at all.

But before we got to that stage we had to learn to be willing to forgive and forget. Sometimes we carry things in our hearts against our children. God helped us to be delivered from this attitude.

What if God was to do us that way; every time we've made a mistake and did something wrong, He would harbor that in his heart; or He would get so mad or angry at us that He would crack us across the head? We'd deserve it if He did, but He doesn't do it that way. He leads and teaches us a lesson in His actions toward us: we should be that way toward others, and especially those of our own family. We have to be loving and kind and understanding. He could have told us: "You can't have any children, I can't trust you to have children." He didn't tell us that. He let us have five beautiful children so he expects us to be parents to them. They don't need us just to tell them when they're good. They need us when they are in trouble too.

From Beverly's problems we learned that as a family we needed to pray together, to love and respect each other.

It has taken some growing up in our children's lives, and a whole bunch of growing up in Mary's and my life, working and dealing with our kids.

Beverly today is the mother of our granddaughter, which we're very proud of. We call her Kee Kee. She's just like her grandpa. Little Kee Kee is the spitting image of Beverly and Otis. Otis is Beverly's husband and is on the Police Department. He's pretty proud of his job. He is a good policeman. We love him and are proud of him.

Our son Irwin is six feet, four inches, weighs 154, and is just skin and bone. I've had a problem relating to him.

I used to love to hunt and fish and I wanted a boy that was going to go hunting with me in the woods, in the muck and mire, and maybe with a shotgun or rifle—killing a few deer or something. I thought I was going to have a fishing partner, or a mechanic partner to help me with the old cars, or to remodel the house.

But not with Irwin. He can keep house better than Beverly, Quincy, Sandra or Marion put together, and was a far better cook than most people.

This disturbed me. I thought, *what am I raising, some kind of a weirdo?*

It was hard for me to relate to Irwin, and yet it shouldn't have been. I should have given Irwin the right to be an individual. God had given to us individual personalities and Irwin's instinct didn't have to be the same as mine. But I wasn't willing to let Irwin be an individual. I tried to mold his life into what *I* wanted him to be. Consequently, Irwin and I grew far apart.

Nevertheless, Irwin began to look for the companionship of a dad, and if he couldn't find it in his dad he would look for it in other things, other fellows. The older guys pushed him around.

Irwin got himself involved in a situation before we moved from Pittsburgh to California. He was in a big fight at his school where there were 2,800 black students. He was working at the time. He had a little job in a grocery store and always had money.

The gang leaders made him pay for his protection. He had to pay a certain amount of money, and if he didn't then he was in trouble. Big, big trouble. If he didn't pay they'd beat him up.

116

When I discovered this I had him transferred to another school.

The teachers didn't believe that Irwin paid for his protection. They weren't to be convinced. I knew Irwin wouldn't lie to me.

When he was transferred to Southside High School in Pittsburgh there was a gang there also—perhaps 40 or 50 kids. Only two or three of them were black. Irwin was going to have to be a part of this gang whether he wanted to or not.

If I had been able to sit down and relate to my son, he could have explained these things to me. I could have maybe been able to help him with his problems. But because I had allowed myself not to relate to him because he was what I considered too weird acting, rather than come to the garage and work on the car with me he would be in the house helping his mother vacuum the floors, when I'd be cutting glass or something. He would rather help his mother than help me. I had to *make* him do things that I thought boys should be doing.

God was going to show me now that it was my fault that I had allowed myself to get so far away from my son. Not because of his reasons or because of his actions, but because I wanted him to do something, or be something that he didn't want to be.

Though he refused to be in the gang, he had to buy pot from them. These kids had a regular chain of pot being sold in the schools and because they found out Irwin worked they made him buy pot. Every week he had to come up with a certain amount of money to buy pot.

I praise God that Irwin never took to smoking pot, nor did he take any heroin, but he had to buy it! He was so afraid he bought it and brought it home and

117

stacked it in his drawer side by side. Each bag of pot was laying there in that drawer. I didn't know any of this.

One day the gang wanted to initiate him into the group. They wanted to make sure that he was going to be a part of that gang so that if they got caught, no matter what happened, that he wasn't going to be on the outside—he was going to be on the "in." If they got caught, they *all* got caught.

His initiation was to go to downtown Pittsburgh to Kuffman's Department Store and steal so much dry goods. Four or five of the boys had been doing this for some time. Irwin was to steal something without getting caught. He went into the store with what I had told all our children earlier in his mind: if you do anything wrong you will wind up eventually getting caught because you can't do wrong and get by. And I would always say that I was a living witness to that statement.

He walked into that store and was looking at two pair of men's pants valued at $30 apiece. He had them across his arms looking at them. The store detective saw him. (He knew Irwin because he had been one of the ushers at Miss Kuhlman's services.) The detective is a Christian. He went immediately, with no hesitation, grabbed Irwin and scared the daylights out of him. He said, "What are you doing, boy?" And with this he took Irwin back to the office and said, "You're stealing those pants and we're going to run you in. We're going to throw the book at you."

They had caught three of the other boys who had stolen a bunch of stuff. These boys had said they were all together, so the detective was ready to run Irwin in with the other boys, at least they made him think so.

They kept him a couple of hours and questioned

118

him. The detective then let him know that he knew me. Then told Irwin to go and call me and have me come to the store and if I came he wouldn't book him. He said, "We can arrest you and you can get six months for this, and if you go call your parents we'll turn you loose into their custody, but you must call them. They've got to come here."

Irwin went out and disguised his voice, called back to the store and said, "I'm Mr. Murphy, I'm busy and I'm tied up and I can't come." But the officer recognized that it was Irwin's voice. Whereas he said, "That's it. I'm going to arrest your daddy and your mama. I'm going to put all you guys in jail because you're all thieves." He was trying to scare Irwin, and he did a good job of it. Irwin then caught the next bus and came home.

Irwin's a six-foot-four kid that eats a lot. When he came from school the normal thing for him to do is to run to the kitchen and just load his arms and go upstairs to his room and eat until his mother got supper ready. He would eat three meals in one afternoon. But this day I noticed he didn't come to the kitchen, he just tiptoed quietly upstairs. We hardly knew he'd come in.

He stayed and stayed there. I said to his mother, "Irwin must be really sick because I don't know any day he's ever come home without him coming in the kitchen. He's got to be sick! I don't even hear him up there."

We called, "What's the matter? Come here."

He said, "I'll be there in a minute," sort of quiet and scarey like.

I thought something is wrong with him.

Finally, he came and said, "Can I see you a moment?"

119

I said, "Yeah, what do you want?"

He said, "Will you come up to my room?" I thought something was really wrong. This kid is really sick, we might have to get a doctor for him.

I went to his room. Irwin had the drawer opened. I didn't notice the drawer at the time cause I never went into his room for anything. It was a typical boy's room. Yet, I should have been going in his room. I should have been talking to my son. I should have had a relationship with him where he could come to me and confide in me. He loved me enough to confide in me, but he was afraid of me. I was some kind of tyrant to him because I was a hunter and a fisherman, I could do all these things: rebuilding houses and mechanics on cars. He couldn't do those things therefore he thought that he was a weakling, (because I told him so) that he was a no-good, that he was a nothing. That he would never amount to anything. (What if God would treat us like that?)

I had turned my son into something he wasn't at all. He had an inferiority complex.

He closed the door that afternoon and broke down sobbing. "Dad," he said, "I got to tell you something and it hurts me to tell you. I don't want to tell you because you'll be hurt by it and I never wanted to hurt you and Mom in any way, but I feel I've got to tell you this, a man's coming out here. This gang at school said I had to steal. I was going to steal some pants, but I got caught even before I started to walk away and this man told me to come and get you. I lied to him by disguising my voice and I told him that I was you and that you were busy and couldn't come down, whereas he discovered that it was me and he's on his way out here to pick you and mama up. He's going to lock us up dad, and I just thought I've got to tell you about it."

Irwin didn't know that the man had called us and said, "Your son is on his way home, and he's got a story to tell you." I thought it was one of his teachers. I didn't know what this thing was all about. Yet, now when Irwin told me this then I realized it was a man from the store, and now I understood what he meant when he said, "Whatever he tells you don't worry about it, all is well." Before I had thought it was his band leader. Perhaps maybe Irwin didn't want to be in band. I didn't understand it. Now it was beginning to make sense.

When Irwin told me again this man was on his way out, I said, "Well, what for?"

He said, "Dad, I did a terrible thing, I was going to steal these pants and, of course, I got picked up, and a man is going to arrest you and mom. He's going to lock us up." It was then Irwin pointed to the drawer and showed me all of this pot stuff that he had been buying for months from those kids at the school.

With this God pointed a finger at me really heavy. "It's because of you" the Lord said to me, "your son has gone this route. It's because of you your son has turned this way. It's because of you your son has felt rejected and has turned to looking for friendship in these other kids, *AND* it will be because of you that your son will turn to me. In spite of you he will turn to me. You are to love your boy. Sit down with him right now and let him know that you love him. Let him talk to you. I put you in charge of this family. You're the head of this home. You're to listen to these children. You're to help them."

I felt so small at this time that I grabbed Irwin. I embraced him.

121

By this time the other members of the family knew what was going on. They were all crying. We loved and hugged each other.

The officer called back and said for me to forget it, he wasn't coming. He knew me and that he knew that Irwin was being framed by these boys and to forget the whole thing.

We began to just love each other and immediately because of this event began an intense prayer for each other. We learned to sit down and listen to each other's problems.

God has opened a tremendous avenue for Irwin James Murphy, my son, to relate to me. Today we have a beautiful relationship.

Irwin went with us to Ireland, and was able to minister to a bunch of kids in an all-girls school there. They had never met a black before. They were all feeling his hair. I wouldn't let them feel mine because mine is moveable, and I didn't want them to touch it. They all loved Irwin. Some of them he was able to pray for and lead them to Jesus—and all of this because I was willing to say, "I'm sorry! Son, forgive me, please. I forgive you."

Chapter 12
Ridiculous Prayer!

It wasn't easy to move from Pittsburgh to our new surroundings. It was difficult to give up the things that we had worked for 14 years to establish: our home, a place in the community, a very lucrative position with the Sunshine Biscuit Company, and to go into full-time ministry.

But it was the best thing we ever did, and the right thing. It was God's choice. It was God's direction. Little did we know at the time all that was going to happen.

In our move we had to give up our home. We could hardly even sell it, we had to almost give it away, we were so in debt at the time.

By the time we got rid of our furniture we had nothing left but the clothes on our backs and a '69 Olds. We had almost no money at all when we left for California. God led every step of the way.

We ministered in Cincinnati, Ohio, on our way out and were given an honorarium. We ministered in St. Louis and were given an honorarium. We ministered in Tulsa, Oklahoma, and by the time we got to California we had several hundred dollars in our pocket, but no place to stay.

Mary was almost resentful that she had to give up all that she had back east and move to a strange place where we had no friends. We didn't know anyone. And yet I knew that the Lord had called me, and that we had to move. There was no way I could stay in the surroundings that I had—those comfortable surroundings where I had allowed sin to come into my life.

This move to California was so directed of God that even when we got to California we moved in with a good brother, Dr. Michael Esses, dean of the school of the Bible. Michael didn't know that we were moving to California permanently. He thought we were just out there to do a meeting in Melodyland, and that we would be leaving in a couple of weeks. When I told him we had made a move and that California was going to be our home, that God had directed me there. He said, "You need a home."

I can understand that—he's got seven people living in his upstairs, so I'm sure he felt that we needed a home!

Then Mike began to pray, and he prayed the most ridiculous prayer. It was a typical Jewish prayer, it went something like this: "Dear God, Willie and Mary got five children and they moved here under your direction, and we know that you wouldn't have them move here unless you had a place for them, so we ask now God that you open a door that Willie and Mary might have a good home here in California. And Lord, don't give them a place in some poverty-stricken area, give them a good home. They're your servants. They are your children. We come to you believing the Word that when we ask anything in Your Name you'll do it. We ask for lodging for Willie."

In the middle of this prayer Mike stopped and

turned to me and said, "Willie, where's your furniture? Is your furniture being shipped?"

I said, "No, we don't have any."

And he started praying all over again, "Lord, let this home be completely furnished." Then he added, "Well, of course, Willie's got five kids, he needs a four-bedroom home. Lord, give him a good four-bedroom home. And they need money. They don't have any down payment for their home, so Lord, you work it out and we trust you to do it, Lord, and we have this blessing because your Word tells us that we do. Thank you, Lord. Amen."

I was relieved when he finished this prayer. I was just tormented while he was praying. I thought, *Well, God won't hear a ridiculous prayer like that. This guy's talking in his prayer, he's not really travailing—he doesn't have the right tone of voice.* It just wasn't the right kind of way to go to God. We all said, "Amen," and I just went, "Oh, wow, praise God."

Little did I know Mike's prayers were getting through to the heart of God. His prayer was the desire of our heart. We wanted this but we just didn't feel that God could answer that fast. We thought that He would give us maybe a little two-by-four house someplace to get started in, and that we had to make it for ourselves. And if the Lord had done it that way it would have been all right with us.

I was used to making it for myself. I wasn't given anything. About everything I've ever gotten, I've had to earn. The Lord has always seen fit for me to have good jobs, and we have earned maybe not all that I *wanted,* but I've earned what we *needed.* Most times we've had to borrow money, but God still let me work so that I could even pay that back.

At the Melodyland Drug Prevention Center there was a hot line where all kinds of job calls come in—people wanting to sell property, etc. Two days after the prayer Mike happened to be walking past the hot line office, a man by the name of George Wakely said, "Hey, Mike, there's a brother over here at the Grand Hotel who is working there who says he has a home, and this home is a four-bedroom house. It's completely furnished. It has a car with it. In fact, he's not even going back to that home and if you know anybody who needs a home you can come over there and pick up the key and go take a look at it."

Nonchalantly, Mike said, "Okay."

That evening when Mike came home he said, "Hey, by the way Willie, there's a key I want you to go pick up. There's a house that we prayed about, I believe it's the house God wants you to have. Go take a look at it."

I thought, *It can't be, it's unreal! God, you didn't do that, did you?*

We picked up this key and went to the house. It was a beautiful home . . . two-car garage . . . four-bedroom . . . avacado trees in the back . . . palm trees and all kinds of flowers and bushes in the back. It was the most georgeous home I'd ever seen. It was beautifully landscaped.

It was in the little city of Orange, and as we looked at it, I said, "This is it. This is our home. We claim this home."

We didn't know at the time that we wouldn't need any down payment. All we needed was the escrow papers to be signed. Of course, that's hard enough, for then we had to be approved too—credit wise. We had very bad credit rating because we were unable to pay our debts on time back in Pittsburgh because of the

126

salary that I was earning, which seemingly just wasn't enough. It was enough but I was disobedient to the Lord and when you're disobedient to Him you can't even manage your money. You can't manage your life. You can't manage anything. And so I got myself in a bind.

When we were looking at this home we didn't know that it was in an all-white section. I didn't know that we'd be the only family living in an area of some 60,000 people and we would be the only black family in the whole area. I didn't know it, and I didn't care. I didn't think about it.

I went back and announced to Mike: "This is the house. I want this house."

I had noticed as we were looking at the house a few of the neighbors came out and were standing around on the sidewalks looking. I didn't pay too much attention. I thought, *They're going to welcome us to the community.*

Well, it wasn't exactly a welcoming party.

One day I was standing outside and one man said to me, "What are you going to be doing here?" I said we were interested in buying. He announced this was a John Birch community.

I was really dumb about these things. I didn't know John Birch or anybody else at this time, so I asked him who was John Birch.

He became very indignant and said, "What do you mean, who is John Birch?" Then gave me a rundown. This was a John Birch community and they didn't have mixed races in this community, and let me know that he thought I would be making a mistake if I were to buy that home.

I told him we were Christians and God had given us the home. With this he was flattened. He said God never gave him anything. Everything he got he worked for. I said, "God gave you the job and he gave you the health and strength that you could work for it." We parted on not-to-good a note.

People called Melodyland where we were attending church and asked, "What was the idea of moving this nigger into our community?"

A few people were indignant about our move into the community, but seemingly the Lord was with us because there was no way we could get the house anyway. I'd only been there just a few weeks, and had no money. I had not credit background in Pennsylvania so I couldn't borrow any money. There was no way this thing was going to go through escrow. Just no way—in the natural. But Mike had prayed a supernatural prayer and God was going to give us a supernatural answer to this prayer to prove to *me* and to no one else, that He had called me and ordained me into the ministry.

He had spoken to me about making that move from Pennsylvania. We didn't know *where* but we were going to move and God showed me California. I had been in California in July, the mountains were all burned up, it seemed like. I didn't see any green grass so I didn't like it. I was used to the tall oak trees, and the rolling green hills.

I signed all the escrow papers, and an attorney friend from Melodyland helped me fill out all the papers. We turned them into the bank. They came back, fully approved. We had that house. We have everything that went with the house!

God moved us into that house within a month. God has blesses abundantly in every way. God would not let me take a salary from any church. He would not let me join a staff of any church, though I probably would have liked to, but He just wouldn't and He proved to me that He loved me, that He had called me into the ministry and that He alone could supply all of my needs as I trusted and depended on Him.

The first week we were in our new home my wife and son got picked up by the Orange Police Department a half dozen times. They would always be approached with: "Your car looked like a car we had on our stolen list." To my son, of course, he "looked like someone they were looking for." They couldn't understand why we would be in that community so they sort of picked on us for a while.

One day I became a little upset when my wife was in the Supermarket shopping and as she came out of the lot, this policeman stopped her and said that it was a big car that she was driving and it looked like the car that had been stolen or involved in the bank robbery. After the fifth approach like this I called the mayor and told him what was happening and that I was really upset about it, and that I wanted this action on the part of the Police Department stopped immediately— this harassing of my family. We were in that community. God had put us there and by the grace of God, we weren't going to leave. We were going to be there and we were going to be neighbors to those our neighbors, and we were going to love everybody in the community. But we weren't going to sit back and be walked on by those who were being disrespectful toward us. And immediately it stopped.

I got a letter from the mayor's department welcoming us to the community.

I received letters and visitation from almost every church in the city of Orange, inviting us to their churches if we didn't have a church home.

129

It was also beautiful in the school system. My son, within six months, became student body president of a school with 2,800 high school students. Marion was a majorette and one of the drill captains.

Irwin became friendly with all the students and they loved him. One day a girl came and wanted to take him to her house where they were having a birthday party for him. Irwin didn't think anything of it. He got dressed, went out and should have noticed that this girl hadn't parked her car in front of our house, but had parked it around the corner from the house. Irwin was just a gullible kid. He went with her and when he got on the corner it was about dusk dark (that's an old southern term, it means the sun's down) and when he stepped around the corner out of these high bushes these six boys with white sheets around them jumped out, they threw a white sheet over Irwin and grabbed him—all six of these football players—and threw him in the back of this car. The car took off screaming wheels, and Irwin, of course, was just as white as the sheets. He was petrified. He was screaming and howling till he almost lost his voice. He thought this was the clansmen and they were after him. They were going to get him now.

After riding around for about two hours they took him to the party where there were about 90 kids waiting and singing "Happy Birthday to him.

We've had all kinds of slanted things happening in our community, but have enjoyed living in Orange County. Our neighbors are just super. The two families we had a little problem with lasted maybe six weeks. Something happened that they moved out of the community. I'm sorry that they were moved out. I would have loved to have had to opportunity just to go to them and love them and let them know that we did love them.

Chapter 13

"You Can't Do That Here!"

I'm learning every day to give praise to my God in every situation. "Whoso offereth praise glorifieth me . . ." (Psalms 50:23).

Because of all the circumstances and all the problems that Mary and I have faced, God is now allowing us to share with others who have similar problems. He's allowing us to love them and to be understanding and to minister to them. In all of this God is teaching us how to praise Him.

There have been many books written on praise and worship. Both are so important in a Christian life.

I'm reminded of King Jehoshaphat and all of the struggles, all of the problems he had, that the family of God got together and they praised God in the midst of their troubles and problems. My family is learning how to do this. When a problem comes up, we're learning just to get together and to worship the Lord, to praise God, to ask God for His understanding and His wisdom. God is meeting us, but seemingly it's through worship and praise that He's dealing with my family.

A group of us went to Sweden and visited 22 cities. The Scandinavian folk are conservative. Shouting and clapping of hands is not the custom.

But worship and praise is so important and if it's done in the power of the Holy Spirit it is in the Spirit, no matter what country one is in.

God inhabits the praises and when He inhabits that means He's right there and when God is right in your midst, beautiful things are going to take place.

We had started off in Stockholm and had some financial problems. Some of the financial responsibilities weren't met, but in spite of all of that we just began to worship God. In every meeting we had an hour of just worship and praise. After this God always met the needs of people spiritually, physically and materially.

We had been ministering some 25 days now, and it was the last day before we were to go home. The travel agency told us that there was an oil shortage and that the backlog of people waiting to go had multiplied, that the planes now had been cut back and that we would perhaps have to stay over an extra month.

We were all very tired when we got this news. It didn't help us any. We had been preaching, worshipping and praising, and we should have known by then that God expected us to *always* live that way. Not only to preach it, but to actually live it.

Sometimes God let's things happen so that He keeps our ears, mind and eyes open to Him.

We had two more services to do. We really didn't want to do those meetings. We were so weary we just wanted to go home. Yet these people were expecting us to minister. Our hearts weren't in it, but we went ahead anyway. It was the wrong attitude. However, we were obedient and went to the meetings.

The meeting in a Lutheran Church was to be held at noon. These people had come together and fixed a large dinner for us. It was perhaps the largest crowd that ever met in that particular church. They came to see these silly Americans, but they loved us enough to fix a huge turkey dinner for us (it was just before Christmas). If we hadn't come we would have disappointed more than 500 people who had come.

It was a fantastic dinner that they had fixed for us, and here we were, of course, out of it. We didn't feel like ministering.

In the meantime we set up all our equipment. Suddenly the rector noticed all the sound equipment set up in the sanctuary. He said to us, "You can't play that here. This church is 111 years old. We've never had this kind of equipment set up in our sanctuary, it will blow the people's minds. You just can't do this."

I told him that we'd been doing it all over Sweden. Why not? We were invited to come and this is what we work with.

"Well, if you use it," he said, "you keep that equipment very quiet, very soft, don't turn it up at all. The volume will just kill the people and they'll be turned off. Don't even mention giving testimonies. If you have something to say just say it, because they won't know what you are talking about. We know how you Americans do. Don't have the people clap their hands because it's not part of our culture. We love the Lord just as much as you Americans do, but it's just things we don't do."

We got into the meeting and started singing "Hallelujah."

In our prayer before the service we had prayed: "Lord, help us, don't let anybody get out of order." We forgot to mention anything about the Holy Spirit, and as we began to sing "Hallelujah" the Holy Ghost

134

began to fall in the meeting.

I looked back at the drummer Paul Johnson. I noticed the Holy Ghost was upon him. Paul had long hair down to his shoulders and when he played his drum sets, he closed his eyes (I couldn't understand how could he see with his eyes closed. Even if he didn't have his eyes closed he couldn't see because his hair would fall over his face), the anointing was coming upon him strongly. He began to kick those drums and the rector had told us: "Don't get loud!"

I thought I'd better break this anointing Paul's getting. Here I am the one who loves to worship and praise because I know that's when God comes and inhabits. Now I'm trying to do just the opposite. (God was going to teach us a lesson even though He'd been teaching us throughout this whole tour and yet He had to come and do it all over again.)

I thought I'd break into this "Hallelujah" and have Paul give a testimony.

The rector had told us, "Don't give any testimonies."

I said to Paul, "Hey, Paul, come give your testimony."

Everybody began to look around. They didn't know what I was talking about.

And then he came with that beautiful anointing all over him, the praise on his lips, with one finger stuck way up (he's about six-foot-six) and began to say "Hallelujah!"

Everybody began to look up to the ceiling of the church, at that up-pointed finger. They didn't know what was coming down on them.

Paul began to tell of how he had been a drug user and at 19 years of age, God set him free from drugs.

135

He played in a rock band, and how he had played! The music had affected his hearing. But God had come and delivered him of this drug problem, and had set him free, made a Christian out of him. He said, "I can't sing them like Willie and Gary (Taski, the leader of the fellowship) and Mike (the guitar player) and Kate Taski (Gary's singing wife), and John and Dale, and the other people, but God has given me this instrument, the drums. I dedicated my drums to Him."

At this point he wheeled around and said, "I've got a song I want to play for you."

I thought, *Oh, Lord, don't let him do it. What is he going to do?*

I didn't know the song he was going to play but Gary Taski had written it—"Jesus Saved Me, I'm So Glad."

When you've been set free by the power of God, when He's come in and liberated you, set you free from bondages of sin, when He sets you free even in your innermost being from all the deep inner hurts and problems, you know you've been set free and you can't keep that quiet. You're not ashamed to tell that to the whole world. These young people had been set free, and they began to sing.

That song is five minutes long. The reason being that Paul has a three-minute long drum solo in it. I didn't know that.

The group began to sing, "Jesus Saved Me, I'm So Glad." All of a sudden it stopped. I thought, *Oh, praise God.* But they stopped so that they could give it to Paul.

Paul went into his act and began to beat those drums. It got so loud I thought the ceiling was going to cave in any minute. Then the group began to shout:

"Jesus Saved Me, I'm So Glad," and he'd beat those drums.

I didn't dare open my eyes. I was praying, "Oh, Lord, forgive us. Forgive because the rector told us not to do this. Forgive Paul for doing it."

I was going to apologize the minute he finished. Seemed like he would never finish. It was like an eternity that he played "Jesus Saved Me, I'm So Glad."

The Spirit of the Lord was on the group. They had been delivered. They had been set free. Gary Taski had said that he was an atheist. Didn't believe in anything. He didn't know anything about Jesus. Now, how can they *not tell* when the Holy Ghost has delievered them from their drug problems and they are set free. They had to be praising God—and they did!

I was just ready to get up and apologize to these people and to that pastor because we had disobeyed him. I thought, I'd grab the microphone and apologize—that's all I can do.

So when I opened my eyes to take the microphone a black woman from Nigeria took the microphone. She was probably 70 years old. She began to prophecy. She put her hand on her side, and I thought she was speaking Swahili. I could tell it was the drum she was talking about because she'd wiggle every other sentence. I thought, *Well, she's just upset about those drums.*

When she finished, a Danish man who had been saved about a month, and only filled with the Holy Ghost about two days prior to that meeting, got up and interpreted in English what she said. I discovered that the woman had prophecied that that church that was 111 years old, had never had anything charismatic in it, never an evangelistic service, didn't even play the organ in it. And now all of a sudden here we were praising

137

God on the high sounding cymbals, the drums, etc.

The man concluded his interpretation by saying that He loves the people who praise Him, and that He was in the midst, that He was able to do anything, even greater than what we were expecting. If anyone needed anything, the Lord would hear, and we would receive from Him."

Those people just became unglued. The stiff-necked people were sitting there like mummies before that. Nobody moved. When I opened my eyes to see what was going on, there wasn't a dry eye in that house. Those people were weeping before the Lord.

I forgot about apologizing. I was caught up in the Spirit also. I was to preach right after that. I gave a very short sermon and read some scriptures about salvation, and commented about the Lord being here with us right *now* and anyone who needed to be saved to stand right where they were.

To my amazement half the church stood. I thought they didn't understand what I was saying. So I repeated it. I had the interpreter (I call them interrupters) repeat it—that only the people who wanted to be saved to stand. Now more of them stood and began to come to the front of the church.

It was the most precious thing I had ever seen in my life. The Holy Spirit was so strong and so real and so pleased with the praise that had come forth from those young people. Not so much from me—I was apologizing. But the Holy Spirit used this loud music of worship and praise to God to touch the lives of those people. And instead of the meeting ending when it should have ended perhaps at 2 or 2:30 o'clock, it lasted until 6:30 that evening.

We forgot about going home. We got caught up in

the Spirit. We began to love those people. A number of them were filled with the Spirit.

When we finished this service at 6:30 we got all the equipment packed and had to rush to the other meeting that was already in progress with 500 Pentecostal Lutheran brothers and sisters who had been touched by Jesus. All had motored and bicycled or walked to this pentecostal church that had wall-to-wall people that night.

The Lord was already moving when we walked in. We took time to set up the equipment. People were sitting in the window sills, every aisle was packed with people.

We began to just worship and praise God. We forgot about going home. All we thought about was giving our God glory. In the midst of the circumstances now, I just said, "Lord, you've got it all. You have it. As to going home, we'll stay here from now till you come if you want us to. It's in your hands."

As the testimonies went out and God's Word went out I saw God move in again. As we worshipped Him a young girl came running to the front. She had a belt around her waist with a place for four or five knives, and said: "I want this Jesus to help me. I'm a gang leader here and I know I'll probably be killed but I don't care. I want this Jesus. I'm a drug user, I want to be set free like these young people have been set free."

We prayed for her. The Lord began to deliver that girl before our eyes and set her free. When she finished we knew that God had touched her because the first thing she did was unbuckle that belt from around her waist and gave it to us. She said, "I don't need this any more. Jesus loves me and I don't need to

139

fight. I don't need to do anything. I'm sick of all of this. I've given it all to the Lord."

All we did was praise God, and the girl too was beginning to praise God. She was expecting the gang to attack her for her stand. But she didn't care. She was going to praise God for His beautiful love and for forgiving her of all her sins, and coming into her life. God moved in a mighty way and many were saved, filled and healed.

When we got back to where we were staying we got a call from the airlines saying "There are eight places on planes going home. We had eight cancellations and we saved them for your team."

Wouldn't you know, God worked it out! In spite of everything, our fears and not wanting to praise Him and love Him.

We can't take praise for what God did in those meetings, God did it all. He gets all the glory for it. We realized that God is sovereign. God loves us. God is concerned about all our needs and problems. All we have to do is realize that He does love us and turn our ways and our cares over to Him.

Sometimes we are so busy fretting over people and their problems. But Psalm 37:1 says "fret not thyself because of evildoers." God has made a promise even to evildoers that He would take care of them. He will see to it that they would have punishment or correction whatever the case may be, but God lets us know that that's His business. We don't have to sit around fretting. We don't have to devise means and ways to destroy a person. We don't have to sit around and assassinate them with our mouths. We are to trust God to handle these situations. We're to praise God. We're to thank God for He knows all things. He has

140

full control of all things.

In Psalm 37:3-6 we are told *what* to do. We are to commit our ways unto the Lord. Not only commit but trust, and to delight ourselves in Him. He will give us the desires of our heart. We are to commit our ways to him and trust him and He will bring it to pass. The word *trust* means for me to throw my cares to my Lord. I can actually cast all my care to Him. I can lean on my Lord. I can throw myself on Him, and as I do this I can trust Him completely knowing that He's the best catcher in the world. He can't miss.

I am learning in my struggles and problems how to throw myself on my Jesus, on His mercies, on His wisdom, on His understanding.

The way gets sweeter and sweeter, and I'm learning to grow and move in the glory of the Lord.

It's exciting to be a Christian. It is the greatest time to be alive. I would have loved to have been alive in Paul's time, but right now is the greatest time. Each day, each challenge just leads me closer to my Lord and makes me love Him more and more. It also makes me love my brothers and sisters more. I don't understand some of them, and I'm sure they don't understand me. God understands us all and He helps us all.

I praise God for the privilege of worship and praise in the midst of problems and circumstances. Everyone of us loves to be praised. The reason for this is that we're built in the image of God. God loves to be worshipped and praised.

After I've been on an evangelistic tour and I go home my wife greets me, and then sets before me a good meal. When I put my heels under that table and begin to chomp on that cornbread, and grease begins to run out of both sides of my mouth, I look at my wife

141

out of one eye and say, "Oh, Mary, this is the greatest dinner Honey. You outdid yourself."

She's sitting across the table from me, waiting for me to compliment her on this dinner and when I do compliment her, she says, "Well, it's just the regular dinner." And yet I can see from the top of her head to the soles of her feet she's eating up that praise. She wanted me to praise her for that dinner. And we're just like God. God loves to be praised.

We are unto God a royal priesthood. We are to show forth the praises of Him who has called us out of darkness into His marvelous light (I Peter 2:9). He has delivered us from sin problems and for this we ought to worship and praise Him.

I received a letter which read like this:

"Hi, Dad. How are you? The reason I'm writing this note is to let you know that I'm always thinking about you. I'm very sorry I didn't get to be with you this time, but you see, Dad, I've been very busy with the talent show and with the presidency position at school. But Dad, when you're away ministering I just miss you and I pray for you. I miss you more and more when you are away. Every night I'm praying for you. I pray that God will use you while you are away. I'm proud to be your son and I thank God for a Dad like you. I'm going to stand as tall as I can to please God and to please you, Dad.

"I don't know if I've ever told you this, nor have I told Mom, but Dad, I love you and I'm saying is now. I really love you and Mom both. My prayer is that God will keep us together as a family and that we will continue the love and peace that we have among each other.

"And as you're away, I hope and pray that God

will use you in the lives of these people to come to know Jesus as their Saviour. Remember this, I'll be praying for you. God bless you. Your son, Irwin."

That's my boy! I popped my buttons when I read that letter.

Irwin should be in the third year in college now and there was not a rightly spelled word on that page, but I didn't need an interpreter for that because that was a praise to me, and it looked like he was writing this in an unknown tongue. But I understood every word of it because he praised me.

God turned that on in me. He said, "All right, you feel that way about your son. What do you think I feel about my children when they do likewise when they praise me?"

Irwin wrote this letter because he loved me. No way would Irwin write. He doesn't write anything to anyone. He had to love me to do that. I knew that.

It wasn't five minutes later, he asked his mother for $2. He got that $2. The next day he came with a piece of paper saying, "Dad, there's a new Duster downtown, I sure would like to buy it. Will you sign for it?" I said, "Son, give me the paper, where do I sign? In fact, you can get two if you want."

God turned that right around and said to me: "Willie Murphy, what do you think about me? You don't praise me so you can get something. You praise me because you love me and you'll get something. If you're in trouble I'll set you free. If you need material things, I'll open doors for you. If you need a spiritual blessing, you're going to get it."

All of this because the Lord inhabits the praises of his people. God just wants to and is just waiting to do something.

143

We're joint heirs with the Son. If for nothing else we should praise God for this.

If you're in trouble, if there's a need that you have and if you are a Christian just stop now and put both your hands in the air, all the way (not half-mast because that means someone is dead) but stick those flags up, really high before God and just begin to worship, just begin to love the Father, not to get something but love Him because He saved you, if nothing else. And the Lord will visit with you. He's with you right now and He'll begin to show you His ways. He'll begin to bring peace to your heart. He'll bring joy. He'll bring contentment. He'll deliver you from your troubles. He will give you the material things you need.

That's our God, but you must be obedient. That is the law of God. If we follow that law God cannot lie, and so we are to give glory to God for the things that He's doing for all of his people right now. Look up and live, and give glory to God!

Chapter 14
A Lesson In Love

One incident that really sticks with me is when my dad and mother went with me from Pittsburgh (where they were living) to Florida where I was to be ordained into the full ministry.

My dad was a loving man and things were going good for them. He had told his people he was going to be off this Sunday, a whole week, because he was going to a big auspicious occasion for his son. (I haven't yet found out what that word means, but evidentally it was something big my dad thought.)

He wasn't used to being around many white people. He would speak to them and then go on his way. He hadn't been able to relate to them, nor had my mother.

But on this week at the Christian Camp they ran into a new experience. Here was this georgeous setting—beautiful flowers, huge birds walking around spreading their wings, the sunshine, temperature at 80 degrees, and all the people had smiles on their faces. Plus, Brother Derstine and all the other good teachers . . . great spiritual food all week.

As my dad sat there God began to speak to him.

Somehow or other, the more education my dad got the more he seemed to come down off of that shouting preaching. God seemed to speak to him and tell him that he was to teach and be quiet in it. Dad got really quiet. Just almost dead. But after being in this camp something happened.

There were some 75 to 100 people (most of them ministers) who came to the altars with my wife and I for the ordination. We knelt before that altar before God, giving our lives into the full ministry. These brothers were praying with us and prophecying over us. The Spirit of the Lord, the anointing of God was so strong. We felt as if we were being raised up off of that floor about six feet. It was really heavy.

My dad was there in the middle of that. Never had he been in that kind of atmosphere in his life. Brother Derstine said, "Now, Rev. Murphy, would you lay hands on Willie. You lay hands on your son and daughter and pray for them that God's blessings come upon them."

The Spirit of the Lord was so high at this moment that when Dad laid his hands on my head to pray for me, God beautifully filled him with the Holy Spirit.

My father went straight up. He never got his prayer out. He went somewhere. He's still floating around somewhere up there with the Holy Ghost and power all over him!

My father is a man who loved Jesus. From the age of six he began to preach the gospel. They would stand him up on boxes, or orange crates behind the pulpit, and people would begin to really get turned on. The Holy Spirit was moving. He didn't know too much about the Word of God, but he had an anointing on his life, and a concern and love for people.

We left that camp driving back to Montgomery, Alabama, after having been gone 20 years.

That Sunday evening I had three hours in Montgomery. I thought, *What can you do in Montgomery? I'll go to church.*

I didn't think about picking any specific church. I didn't know any particular one. I thought, *I'll just go to the first one I see.*

While driving near the Danley Field I saw this beautiful, big church . . . seating probably 2,000. Busses were lined up all around it. I could hear the music from the outside.

I parked a couple of blocks away and ran back to the church. I just wanted to get in and be there that night. I felt so good in the Lord, in the love of God, and I thought I had everything I needed. I didn't need any more from God. He'd done everything that week. I was a full-time evangelist now, an ordained minister so I could light this whole world. I had all the love of God in me, I thought.

When I got to the front door of this church I was met by one of the deacons who was getting ready to light his cigarette.

I said, "Sir, you got a meeting going on here?"

"Oh," he said, "we have the biggest meeting we have ever had in our church. We have a group of singers and our church is packed. I just wanted a smoke, I'm going right back."

"Well," I said, "is it an open meeting?" I wasn't thinking race-wise, I just wanted to know if one had to pay.

He looked at me and said, "Oh, you're black, aren't you?"

I don't know where he got that idea!

"I guess so, I'm black," I replied.

"Oh, I'm sorry," he said. Took his cigarette, threw it down, began to smash it with his foot and said again, "I'm sorry. You know our government is changed, the blacks and whites work together in the school system, even the post office, but unfortunately, we just haven't worked those problems out in our church yet, consequently we don't mix the races or the congregations here in our church. We just don't mix them, and I can't invite you to this meeting tonight."

"But," he said, "I'll take you across town where you can go to church."

I thought, *Man, this is strange. What does he mean: take me across town to a church?*

I had just left the camp all filled with the Holy Ghost and the love of God. I thought my God would point a finger at that man and say, "Get out of here. Willie's going into that church." But God didn't.

God let me know that I, Willie Murphy needed more of Him. That I needed more love because the minute that man said he couldn't invite me in I had the thought, *I'm going anyway. I can go into the church. I'm free.*

God stopped me cold in my tracks and said, "Willie Murphy, do you love me?"

That's all I could hear, a quiet still voice: "Willie Murphy, do you love me?"

I said, "Yes, Lord, you know I love you, but what about this guy?"

He said, "I didn't ask you about that fellow. I asked you about you."

I was so busy pointing my finger at the churches, and at the people that I didn't take time to see that there were errors in my life that God needed to do some more work on. I still had prejudice in my heart. Maybe it wasn't as deep as it was before, but it was there and God needed to work some more in my life. I knew this was so for when the man said, "I'll take you across town," I said, "No, Sir, that's all right, I'll find a church." I said it unkindly.

And with this I turned and walked away. As I got in the car I heard again, "Willie Murphy, do you love me?"

I was beginning to be a little up tight with God because I knew He knew I loved Him.

I'd been all over the world ministering in churches. I didn't ask to go to white churches to minister, that's where God placed me. For the past years ninety-nine percent of those churches were all white. Out of 200 churches perhaps four a year had been black churches. I thought I was loved among all the people, and now God was asking me, "Do you love me?" I thought, *What a question. God knows I love Him.* But God knew that I needed more, and He was going to do a job on me.

"You know I love you, Lord." But He kept asking me. He wouldn't stop.

Finally, I said, "Lord, I love you, but I sure need some more of your love tonight."

And God says, "That's what I was waiting for you to ask me, for more love."

When He said that I couldn't even start the car. All I could say was, "Lord, forgive me. Forgive me for being arrogant with that man. I'm sorry Lord. Lord, let the Holy Spirit fill me with love. I need to go to church. Help me so I won't be bitter toward anyone whether I'm invited or not."

The Lord heard me and beautifully and sweetly the

149

Holy Spirit began to tenderly touch me all over. I became warm. I can't put into words how I felt in those few seconds as the Lord dealt with my heart.

I started the car and took off for some black churches. I thought I knew where they were located, but come to find out they were all closed on a Sunday evening. I suppose they had done a good job Sunday morning and they didn't need to come back Sunday night. I was hoping to find some church where for just a while I might be ministered to.

I found a church in downtown Montgomery. I got the same response: "We can't invite you in, but we'll take you to a church . . ."

I was a little up tight with these guys telling me that they can't invite me in and then wanting to take me to another church. I thought, *For God's sake man, I'm at a church. Why are you going to take me to another one?*

I left abruptly and drove to the third church. This time two guys said, "No, you can't come in here. We don't have blacks meeting at this time. We have a black group come in at 2 o'clock because they don't have a church, but we don't mix these congregations. No, you can't come in."

This incident nearly unglued me, but God redeemed the whole situation by pouring His love over me. As I turned to walk away, I found myself saying, "That's all right sir, Jesus loves you and so do I." Then I heard this soft voice of the Lord saying, "Willie, you were worrying about getting into those churches. Don't you realize I've been trying to get into some churches for 50 years?" I just had to smile, and I said, "Thank you, Lord, for your love."

As I entered into the car I prayed, "Lord, give us all more of your love."

AS TOLD BY JOY DAWSON:

To say that I had an unusual introduction to Willie Murphy is the understatement of the year . . .

I was sitting at the head table of the Women's Aglow luncheon meeting in Pittsburgh, October, 1975, thoroughly enjoying the program, prior to bringing the message, when the chairwoman spotted Willie Murphy in the audience of approximately 600 people. She spontaneously invited him to come to the microphone and lead in some singing.

I had never seen Willie before and knew nothing about him. After he had led us in some worship songs in that inimitable, warm, infectious style, he paused to tell us of a recent experience he'd had in one of the southern states.

One Sunday evening during his travels as a singer and song leader, he found himself without any commitments in a large city. Desiring to worship the Lord, with the Lord's people, he went to a church, only to be told when he got to the door that they were sorry but they didn't accept blacks in their church.

He went to another church, and was told the same thing.

Undeterred he tried a third church, only to be turned down at the door again.

After that he gave up and went back to his hotel room. I listened incredulously. I remember thinking, "If I were not hearing this man say this personally I'd find it hard to believe."

Willie hastened to exhort the audience who were reacting in amazement, sorrow, and disgust, that we were not to think badly of the people in those churches, and repeatedly said, "I'm sure

151

they're all God-fearing people."

There wasn't a hint of bitterness in his spirit toward those people, as he went on to tell us that as he walked away from the third church, the Lord spoke to him and said, "Willie, you need more love for me". . . . His response was a thoughtful, "Yes, Lord, that's right. I do. And I want more love for you."

As I listened to the honesty of this man, my dear brother in Christ, and sensed the absence of self-pity, and resentment, my reaction was one of great compassion to him for the unjust hurt he'd received from some of my brothers and his—our Christian family.

Then I started to think that the need of the Christians who had rejected him was far greater than his. How far away from the truth in I Corinthians chapter one, verse 2 they were. "Called to be saints, together with all those who in every place call on the Name of our Lord Jesus Christ, both their Lord and ours," and Colossians chapter one, verse 4 . . . "we have heard of your faith in Christ Jesus and of the love which you have for all the saints . . . ."

I grieved for their greater need.

After that, my thoughts went toward God the Father, and I realized that His heart was hurting the most. As I pondered on this, He gave me the clear understanding of what I was to do in relation to Willie.

By this time Willie was back in the audience and the program continued. As soon as the meeting was handed over to me I asked Willie to come up and stand beside me. I immediately put my arm around him and said, "The Lord has spoken to me and said, "Because you were rejected publicly three times, you are to be acknowledged and received with love publicly." And in obedience to the Holy Spirit I took Willie's face in my hands and kissed his cheeks three times and each time said, "I love you, I love you, I love you."

Willie was overwhelmed with the love of God toward him and kept repeating over and over, "Thank you, Lord Jesus."

The audience of approximately 600 people spontaneously stood to their feet, and clapped and clapped and clapped and praised the Lord vocally.

Then came a strong clear message in tongues from someone in the audience.

I called the people to be in prayer and faith that God would give the interpretation of that message to someone according to I Corinthians 14:5, 13, 26-27.

The Lord answered by putting the following words into my mind: "Then shall all men know that you are my disciples because you have love one for another. Oh, my people, I yearn for the day when you will understand the prayer of my Son as He prayed to me that the world would know that I had sent my Son and that I love you as I loved my Son. This will be the mark that will draw all men to me and it is the enemy's attempt to keep from this fulfillment of the prayer of my Son to me that causes these things to happen, to divide, but it will be love that will be the thing that will win through and is the greatest aid to world evangelism and I am pleased as you today stand here demonstrating that you are truly one in Jesus."

Again we all turned our hearts to the Lord and spontaneously worshipped Him for breaking through amongst us.

Needless to say, my heart has been uniquely knit to dear Willie Murphy ever since. It was not long after that experience that I had the further joy of meeting and expressing my love to his dear wife Mary.

153

Editor's note:

The following is taken from a photo album sent to Willie in appreciation for his ministry among a group in Pittsburgh. The album was filled with photos of the various camp incidents, along with the "note" to Willie.

HAPPINESS IS KNOWING WILLIE

What do you remember about Willie?

As the question was asked invariably the answer came back—LOVE!

Willie, in all that you do there seems to be that touch of God's love. We, Gastonville M.Y.F., can remember many special times with you—and P.T.L. we're part of your family. As you have lived with us, worked with us and helped us in so many ways—surely we've seen God's hand extended.

From our seats high in the balcony of Syria Mosque, at the Dave Wilkerson rallies, we couldn't tell what you looked. like, but every month Kathryn Kuhlman would say, "Come on, Willie, sing that song, 'Every Time I Feel the Spirit' again for us." It was such an appropriate song. We felt the Spirit.

Willie—just a name, just a voice, little did we realize how special you would become to each of us.

When we were invited by Jim Inks to go and hear the "McCrary Five" at the Methodist Church in downtown Pittsburgh we didn't know that the "Willie" we had heard sing at Syria Mosque would be there. As we trooped in, late as usual, we could feel an excitement in the air, but more than that, we could feel *love!!—God's love!* For the first time we got a good look at "Willie," and even though the audio system was bad and we couldn't hear too plain, we could sense the LOVE you had for your God. We left the church that night with our spirits lifted and with a new-found friend.

This was the beginning of many rallies we were to attend where you and the "McCrary Five" would be singing.

154

As the group has the characteristic habit of coming LATE and staying LAST you surely had to notice us because of the FIRST habit, and couldn't avoid us because of the LAST. Thus started a friendship that because of Christ, will last forever.

Trips to see you have been many, but some have a unique way of standing out. Youngstown: via Wheeling (Oh, no!). We weren't late for the service, we arrived AFTER it ended. Despite this you thrilled us by singing for us.

Even better were times when you came to visit us. First, programs with the McCrary's at Gastonville church sure did liven things up—especially with Sammy coming as the program ended. Then you alone adding your special touch to a few Sunday morning services—and *everyone* loved you!

Hey, Willie, can you come out Thursday!? How well we remember those prayer meetings. You brought your friends to share with us. We especially remember the Catholic kids from St. Paul, and Ruby. Later we visited St. Paul's prayer meeting, and also attended a prayer meeting at Ruby's. Our only complaint, you were never with us enough.

Camp '69. You are going to camp with us for the first time. You and the Rev. chose the same theme and already the Holy Spirit was moving. First Corinthians 13 was the chapter, and who there will ever forget learning about and experiencing God's divine love.

Cabins were assigned and no one realized the significance. It wasn't until much later we discovered the deep lessons that were being learned and the reason for the special closeness that developed between you and members of the group.

You taught the (dare they be called) younger ones classes in Mohawk Lodge and on the bus. Influence of these lessons was seen in continuation of discussion and—what about the boys' cabin class on Corinthians at 3:30 in the morning? Your involvement extended far beyond the teaching sessions as you spent hours talking with each of us helping with questions and problems. Patty Slayzak was born again—making the whole weekend worth while—Tommy Lythe became so very special to you—Martha was, and still is, your 13-year-old. With each of us it seemed you could tell if something was wrong, and we couldn't help being touched by your concern and love.

It was your first time at the service at Seneca, and we still remember you and the Rev. practicing your songs on the bus—then the beautiful way the Holy Spirit anointed your playing and singing at the rock. After the service you hiked out to the road with us, leading the singing all the way.

As the Holy Spirit took over at Camp '69 we were tremendously blessed and each person was drawn into a perfect bond of love—for those hours at camp we knew the unity of the Spirit.

We remember many of the good times since then that you and our "group" have shared. You came with us as we sang at different churches, Hill Station, Monongahela Baptist, Methodist Church in Jones' Mill, and can we ever forget Belview Baptist Church. Willie soon learned our difficulty with time and ably covered for us there when we got lost and were late, late. We got lost at the Liberty Tubes when all five cars (and only one with the directions) went into the city different ways. But, as always, the Lord was faithful and reunited us on the North Side. We also remember how well Jimmy Kotow played for you—he seemed to get a special touch as you did the favorite songs. Truly we are a family, and the Spirit brought us even closer as we worked together for the Lord.

We taught each other songs. How many times have we sung, "I Will Serve Thee," and who doesn't enjoy you singing, "Sweet Holy Spirit"? You did your first record and we so enjoyed it as the songs have special meaning to us. We needn't mention the second record as each has one at home with grooves worn down to practically nonexistence.

"Sunshine Willie." Why was it that after meetings we never could remember the name of your company? You always caught us with Nabisco cookies on the table. Your favorite quip was, "Hey—what is this???" And going on to expound on the superiority of Sunshine cookies.

Christmas just won't be the same this year with part of our family, you and Mary, missing. This was one night we looked forward to being together to share this most holy night. We remember how beautifully you sang, "Silent Night," during the candlelight service.

The holiday season also reminds us of the impression you made New Year's Eve at the Monongahela Baptist Church. Always a sharp dresser, that night you had on a purple crushed-velvet coat—WOW!! Remember Rev. Sommers said you looked good enough to eat. This was also the night your car quit and it was Danny to the rescue!

We will always remember you doing your best to help us. At our February Retreat, which was held for the Baldwin kids, even though you were sick and very tired, you were with us. We recall the final wrap-up session on Sunday afternoon when again you and the Rev. worked so well together to reach the most difficult ones. How smoothly the Spirit worked. The Rev. said the right words—you sang, to make a crooked path of confusion straight, and very clear. And we learned the value of setting the example by "living the life." (We hope.)

You were true to your promise about Camp '70, and we found ourselves together again at Cook's Forest. Each camp different, yet following a pattern. The Holy Spirit again worked. Especially memorable was Jackie, Saturday night when she glowed and laughed with joy under the Spirit's touch. Others made decisions for Christ as the Holy Spirit used you and Bill Bair in the classes and prayer meetings.

We always were blessed when we prayed for you, as we made a circle inside Mohawk Lodge that last Sunday—again we felt the closeness. One could also sense the depth of your relationship with Christ as you faced the important upcoming decisions about your ministry.

That next year did bring major decisions. As you became busier in your ministry we saw less and less of you. We heard stories of trips you were taking across the country. It was impossible to get you on the phone before one a.m.—if then. More frequent were the conversations with Mary—busy keeping the "home fires burning." Our complaints, however, are vastly diminished as we hear the reports of how God is using you across the country.

This spring, '71, you promised to be with us once more at camp, and this time we really gave you some work to do. Sixty-one kids at Laurelville—a far cry from Cook's Forest. Many, many lessons were learned, not the least of how powerful is the enemy. We remember classes on Galatians 5:16, and also the service Saturday evening when the Holy Spirit once again moved at Camp. At Laurelville you almost lost your song-leader position. Timmy (your six-year-old) kept practicing from the balcony.

So, with summer and fall comes the news that you and your family are being moved to California. And for us that means a time of looking back—remembering all the happy times with you, and also the serious times when important decisions were made by a person whose life is dedicated to God's service. We also take time to realize what our relationship means. That we are a family united by an unending divine love. Our friendship and familyship can never end. The closeness can't be lost by distance, and we can only look forward to many future times of fellowship with you.

These pages only begin to tell what you have meant to us. We have looked to you for inspiration, teaching and prayer, and won't try to list the many times members of our group have received help and encouragement from you.

As you sing we've seen you touched by God's LOVE— then our spirits came alive as we felt that love. As you worked with us we've seen the concern and love God has given you for each of us. And as we thank God for His LOVE, we also give thanks to Him for bringing you into each of our lives.

We pray that God will continue to use you—filling you daily with His *abundant love.*

Willie, we love you, and hope to see you as often as your work brings you back to Pittsburgh.

Your family,
Gastonville M.Y.F.

Chapter 15

Highlights
by My Wife Mary

I met Willie when we were just teen-agers in senior high school.

His dad being a Methodist minister was sent to our small town in Alabama to pastor for two years. Willie was the only one of four boys left at home, so he had to come along. When the word got around all the girls went crazy over him . . . except me. He was the talk of the town. I thought he was ugly and silly. As time went on and I got to know him then I didn't think he was so bad. I wasn't interested as I had a boy friend.

I had three brothers and Willie started to come visit them and began to look at me and pick at me. My mother loved him, so I began to talk to him. He was so nice—different from all the other teen-age boys around. So, I began dating him. After a while we fell in love. After graduating from high school we were married, left Alabama and moved to Pittsburgh.

We joined a Methodist Church. We thought we were Christians. We had been married three years when Willie began to go to Kathryn Kuhlman meetings. It was then we found out we had to be born again, that we needed to accept Jesus in our hearts and in our lives.

160

This changed our total lives.

We gave up our church, and most of our friends turned away from us. Not because of Jesus but because we were going to hear Miss Kuhlman. That didn't change us for we knew she was for real, and the One she talked about made us feel alive. God gave us new friends, and we began to grow in the Word of the Lord.

Our family began to increase and increase until there were five. Willie worked very hard trying to make a living for me and the kids. He sang in the Kuhlman choir, some group singing, and some solo work in various churches. He was very busy. Seemingly more so every day. I stayed home most of the time with the children. He always shared with me the happenings at work, choir, etc.

We were just like any other young couple. We had our problems—our ups and downs. More downs than ups—but we knew Jesus and we knew He would bring us through, and He did.

After fifteen years in the Kuhlman choir Willie received the Holy Spirit under Dr. Jarman's ministry. That brought a change in our lives—one I did not understand. I was happy doing what we were doing all those years. Willie was going out more and more singing at weddings at other churches.

After being in the Kuhlman choir ministry for eighteen years he said the Lord had called him into full time ministry. That just went in one ear and out the other for me, but he meant it. He was going to give up the Kuhlman ministry and his job also. I thought he had flipped mentally.

The Charismatic Movement had just begun. Things began to happen. He was asked to lead the singing at the Pittsburgh Conference and from that time people began

161

to call him and ask him to come to their church. He went to other conferences and conventions across the country, getting busier all the time.

The next year he was asked to lead the singing again at the Pittsburgh Conference. Many of the guest speakers came to our home for dinner. After the serivces one night Dick and Bettye Mills came home with us. That night they prayed that I might receive the Holy Spirit.

What joy and peace came over me! My eyes were opened and I could understand why Willie wanted to to and tell others about Jesus and his love.

Willie had gone to California for the Melodyland Clinic. From there he called me and said he was definitely going into the ministry full time. I replied: "Okay, if that is what you think the Lord wants."

Then I wondered *Why did I say Okay?* It was the Holy Spirit who spoke through me. The only thing I could think of was: *How are we going to pay the bills and feed the five children?*

The Lord provided and took care of us as Willie travelled with the "Video Advantage" for a year. After that fell through we were really on our own.

Willie got involved with a group seeking to start a hot line. I didn't get involved because I didn't feel that was what the Lord wanted for us. It was the worst time of our married life. We were fighting the call of the Lord and wanted to do our own thing.

Things were just not working out. Willie blamed me and I blamed him. We came to the point where it had to be what Jesus wanted for our lives. We prayed together as a family for God's direction. He showed us that He had great plans for our lives if we were ready to follow Him. We finally said, "Yes, Lord."

162

Through a good friend God gave me the scripture
Zechariah 2:5: "For I, saith the Lord, will be unto her
a wall of fire round about, and will be the glory in the
midst of her." And another scripture from Isaiah 32:18:
"And my people shall dwell in a peaceable habitation
and in sure dwellings, and in quiet resting places." (And
Proverbs 3:33, and my very favorite, Job 34:29).
Praise the Lord!

Being Willie's wife and the mother of our five
children is the greatest gift that the Lord has given me.
Even though there is not always a smile on his face
and a song in his heart, I'll still chase him for a husband.
I thank the Lord for giving him the love and the
patience to put up with me as his wife. It has been a
great twenty-five years!

We are all living in a time when family, social,
financial, physical, political and spiritual pressures are
pressing in on us from all sides. If we stand in our own
flesh and try to meet them, it is not long before we
find our backs against the wall.

Through troubles and trials Willie and I found out
that we can still wear a smile, because our God watches
over us. In our twenty-five years of marriage we have
had many obstacles but our God has always been there.
Some of our problems are so small that we don't want
to bother the Lord with them and some of them are
so large that we are unable to hand them over to Him.
We think we are stuck, but the Bible tells me a different
story. Acts 12:8 says that God cares for the small details
of a man's life when he reminds Peter to "Gird thyself,
and bind on thy sandals."

Praise God for His forgiveness and understanding.
When we go to God and ask for anything and our

motives are right when we ask, it shall be done. So if you need to be forgiven speak to Jesus about it and it is done and you can wear a smile (Romans 8:35). The devil cannot even accuse us or even remind us of our past. Praise be to Jehovah.

Since moving to California five years ago, the Lord has done many things in our lives. We have had the opportunity to do a great deal of traveling in our country and other parts of the world. Our first trip out of the country was a world tour to Tokyo and Hong Kong where we had some fantastic meetings. We saw God meet many needs also in Singapore, Indonesia, Bangkok, Bombay and New Delhi, from Iran to Tel-Aviv, the Holy Land.

We just praise the Lord for allowing us to minister in those countries and many others. Each day with the Lord is exciting as we wait upon him. On another trip we had a chance to minister in Ireland and London where we saw hundreds of people worshiping and praising God. One meeting started at 2:00 in the afternoon and lasted until 10:00 o'clock at night as the words of Christ brought joy and peace to many hearts, as well as ours.

As the months and years swept by, the Lord led us to minister in many different cities, large and small, throughout the United States and overseas.

The cry of the people is still the same wherever we would go. People from all areas of life are searching, some not even sure for what, and others knowing the fulness of the Lord just coming to draw more from the precious anointing that God pours out on His people when all come together to worship and praise in Jesus' name.

Praise God for the opportunity He has given us

here in America to be free and open in our worship. We often forget that in many countries the people must meet secretly before they dare mention the Bible or utter the precious name of Jesus.

What an inspiration and joy it has been to meet and fellowship with all the wonderful people all over the world. We praise God for the spiritual and financial support that our brothers and sisters have given us.

As we look back we could see the Lord leading us into a new outreach of ministry. In April of 1976 Willie was installed as one of the pastors at Omega Center in Santa Ana, California. We could see that the Lord would have us reduce our travels, but certainly not to cut them out entirely. Willie still plans to minister in different states and overseas as the Lord leads, but we can see that the needs are the same in Orange County as around the world.